Unlocking Me

THE GUIDE TO CREATING
POSITIVE CHANGES IN YOUR LIFE

INEZ SOBCZAK

NEW YORK

LONDON • NASHVILLE • MELBOURNE • VANCOUVER

Unlocking Me

The Guide to Creating Positive Changes in Your Life.

Published in New York, New York, by Morgan James Publishing. Morgan James is a trademark of Morgan James, LLC. www.MorganJamesPublishing.com

Proudly distributed by Publishers Group West®

Morgan James BOGO™

A **FREE** ebook edition is available for you or a friend with the purchase of this print book.

_____

CLEARLY SIGN YOUR NAME ABOVE

Instructions to claim your free ebook edition:
1. Visit MorganJamesBOGO.com
2. Sign your name CLEARLY in the space above
3. Complete the form and submit a photo of this entire page
4. You or your friend can download the ebook to your preferred device

ISBN 9781636981420 paperback
ISBN 9781636981437 ebook
Library of Congress Control Number: 2023931669

Cover Design by:
Rachel Lopez
www.r2cdesign.com

Interior Design by:
Christopher Kirk
www.GFSstudio.com

Morgan James is a proud partner of Habitat for Humanity Peninsula and Greater Williamsburg. Partners in building since 2006.

Get involved today! Visit: www.morgan-james-publishing.com/giving-back

This book is dedicated to anyone who is still suffering in silence.

TABLE OF CONTENTS

INTRODUCTION

For a lot of years, I really thought I had everything under control. I was an achiever: physically fit, successful in business, and the life of the party on my downtime. If you could have it all, I did.

Never mind that anxiety crawled the walls of my heart from time to time. Never mind that there were whole blocks of memories that were closed to me: sheer black walls in my mind. Never mind that my personal relationships were suffering, and friends were stepping back because I was too much.

Never minding almost killed me.

When you don't mind things, they don't go away. They grow bigger and heavier until they make you pay attention. They stop your life in a way you can't ignore.

It took me several years and a chain of personal lows to reach the point where I began to heal for good. On the way to my healing, I dealt with this habit of suppressing what I truly felt and who I truly was. Growth and peace for me today look like awareness and wholeness.

And that's what I hope I can share with you. As I share my life story, I'll point out the steps I took to unite parts of me that had been divided. I'll show you how I invited all of the hard things to show up, be seen, and take a seat.

Giving them a seat means they're no longer in my way. Seeing where they are means they can't slink around and trip me up. Only by looking at the darkness in my life could I make way to walk into the light. And that's where I am now.

To remember my moment of decision always, I got a tattoo that reads: Fall 7 Rise 8. And I truly believe that possibility with all my heart! No matter how many times life trips you up, no matter how many times you taste asphalt, if you get back up, you win.

Let's start your win right now.

When you don't mind things,
they don't go away.

No matter how many times
life trips you up,
no matter how many times
you taste asphalt,
if you get back up, you win.

FOUNDATIONS

From my earliest moments, I toddled through trage-
dies that could have broken me forever. But even in
those moments, I find elements of strength, moments
of grace. I find meaning that I can hold when life gets hard—
truths about who I am that will never change.

As I share these moments in my life, I challenge you to
look at yours. Where do you come from? Who are you at the
core? Where can you find strength in your hard places?

Heritage

One of the true things about me is something that you can see in
my name at birth: Inez Esperanza Valdez. If you can't narrow
down the heritage past Latina, that's okay. But my name pro-
claims me as Cuban. That's an identity that has meant different
things to me at different times in my life, things I'll share as
we go along.

Today, being Cuban means that I'm strong, both body
and soul. Genetically, I can build a lot of muscle in my lower
body, giving me a solid foundation. That's important to me as
a bodybuilder and as a fitness coach.

Historically, I know that I come from an island of people
who have fought for freedom and who have suffered at the

hands of strong and selfish men. They don't give up, and despite the hard moments in their history, they still know how to make the best of what they have and how to enjoy life.

Personally, being Cuban means that I bring some of the flavor of that island with me into my daily life. Like my homeland, I'm warm and full of life. Dancing and music breathe life into me. And I find that the practical and the spiritual coexist within me deeply.

I also find some true things about me in my name. Maybe you have looked through baby books or had an older relative explain to you what your name means. I have learned that my first name, Inez, means Purity. My original middle name, Esperanza, means Hope.

These names explain some vital things about my story. I grew up in a culture that assumed a lot of negative things about my character because I came from brown people. People in charge of my life assumed that I couldn't possibly be pure, and their expectations never left me.

I found that I tried so hard to be pure in a lot of ways, ways like perfect grades, volunteering, physical strength, and social popularity. Some of those attempts were more successful than others. But generally, the attempts to fulfill someone else's expectations brought me pain.

What brought me peace is realizing that my soul is pure. I don't have to do anything to wash it clean or straighten it out. Human souls are pure and precious because they are human, because they are the part of us that can touch the divine.

And that's where my middle name comes in. Esperanza—Hope—is meaningful to me because without Hope, I would not have kept rising again, trying again, and believing that the next time I tried would be the one that worked. You know, if you keep telling yourself that message of hope, you will eventually be right.

Abandonment

Here's the story I grew up knowing. My mother, a Cuban immigrant to Miami, strayed to the wrong side of the law. She fell in love with Oscar, a handsome, charismatic, sometimes violent man who was involved in drugs. My mother became addicted and engaged in some activities that would eventually land her in prison. She had two children while she was with this man: me and my brother Ronald, who was eleven months younger than me.

When Ronald was a baby and I was one, my mother left Ronald and me with a babysitter. I heard a story somewhere while I was growing up that she was going for a pack of cigarettes; I don't know if that's true. What is true is that she never came back. Eventually, the babysitter called social services.

It's scary that I don't have a memory of my mother prior to her leaving me. But the trauma of recalling what I lost when she left has kept those memories dormant. As a one-year-old child, I was already protecting my psyche from the trauma of being abandoned by my birth mother.

After my mother did not return, the sitter called social services. That phone call began my three years of foster care. During those three years, I lived in twenty-six homes. The dramatic lack of stability I faced as a baby just stuns me every time I let myself think about it. And to compound the feeling of isolation and lostness, Ronald and I went to different foster homes. We didn't see one another for years.

Raised by a series of strangers, I learned early that I had to earn my keep. I had to be quiet—so hard for an active little girl like me! And I had to help out. Luckily, my natural energy helped me with this one. I learned how to clean and tidy a space before most kids learned their ABCs.

I also learned that if I made somebody mad or did something wrong, even if I didn't understand what I was doing, men in black police uniforms and women in suits would show up, pack up me and some of my things, and take me to strangers. It was a hard, painful, permanent lesson.

These repeated moves in my young life also influenced any future interactions with police. Before I could understand why, I formed a sense memory of police as people who took you away from your home and gave you to strangers. For the rest of my life, the sight of a police uniform would make me afraid, deeply sad, and unable to speak, just as the toddler version of me had been unable to speak during these transitions.

A lot of times, people focus on the miracle of adoption, how the child is chosen by the adoptive parents and how life is so much better than it would have been if the child had remained in an abusive situation or state care. That side of the story is true, yet it is also incomplete.

For a child to be removed from birth parents is never the ideal situation. Even in cases of abuse or neglect, there is a real bond of blood and belonging between parent and child, and when it is severed, there is grief. To ignore that grief, reminding the child to be grateful and happy for the new family, is to cover an unhealed wound. The infection has nowhere to go but inside.

I learned from mental health and productivity expert Dr. Julie Lopez, whose book *Live Empowered* is a tremendous resource, that adopted children are more likely to suffer from substance abuse. They are four times more likely to commit suicide than the general population. They are seven times more likely to need some kind of mental health therapy.

All these statistics point to the fact that there is some real hurt that needs to be seen and addressed while the child is growing up. To point only to luck and the future is to tell half the story. That's not what I'm here to do.

With that said, my entire foster care experience was not negative. The last home I remember before being adopted is the Brown family. Like many of the foster parents that took me in, Mrs. Brown was a large, buxom Black woman, and I liked living with her. I imitated her way of speaking and moving and drank in her general air of sass and confidence. I associated Black women with warmth, acceptance, order, and strength mainly because of her.

I picked up my need for a spotless house from Mrs. Brown. There is even a picture of me when I was little with a little white hanky pinned to me. Her house was spotless because all the children she fostered or kept in her care were charged with keeping that house spick and span. Mrs. Brown could be mean if you didn't do what she told you to do.

She wasn't mean to me because I did what I was told. I also learned early how to change myself to fit within any group, a lesson ingrained in me by the time I was adopted by the Sobczaks. Oddly enough, Mrs. Brown lived just a few blocks away from the parents who would adopt and raise me.

This transition, while it was only a few blocks of space, was a huge one for me. My constant moving and adapting to strangers was going to stop. Instead, I was going to have to learn how to be part of one unique family. They were not a blank slate, and neither was I. We all had some adjustments ahead.

Adoption

The people who raised me, Mike and Barbara Sobczak, had lived in Miami most of their lives. They both loved Miami in the sixties and seventies, back when the city was safe. They met while they were in high school. They were both Catholics, both pretty even-tempered, both from large families, and both very family-oriented. The two of them turned out to be a good match.

Dad worked his way up the ladder in the medical field. With his logical mind and huge heart, medicine was the perfect career field for him. He started out working as an orderly in the nuclear medicine department of a hospital, and he worked to earn the education and certifications he needed to handle more and more important jobs in the hospital. By the time I joined the family, Dad had a great job working at Miami Heart Institute as a nuclear cardiologist.

Meanwhile, Mom worked a few jobs after high school. But as soon as my sister Meredith was born, Mom became a full-time mom at home. Mom and Dad's first child, Meredith, had my dad's dark hair and eyes and my mom's quiet disposition. Mom and Dad were loving, devoted parents who prized this first child and wanted more. But no other babies arrived to complete the family. So, Mom and Dad took the classes to become foster and adoptive parents.

Meredith was excited at the possibility of siblings. She was six years old and couldn't wait to share her home and her parents with some other kids. I'm thankful for this heart she had. She opened her life to me in a genuine way from the very beginning.

The first other kid my parents found to adopt was my birth brother Ronald, so winningly handsome with his light brown hair and hazel eyes. He suffered from asthma, just as Meredith did, and so my parents knew how to help him. He fit right in with the Sobczaks.

When Mom and Dad took Ronald in, the social workers told them, "You know, he has an older sister who is also in foster care."

"We'll take her," Mom said. "They should be together. You can go and get her now."

God bless Mom and Dad for this impulse. If Ronald had landed with another family, they might not have chosen to adopt me, too. And I cannot imagine life without my brother, who is closer to me than almost anyone else. However, our welcome to the Sobczak house was not easy.

After I came to the Sobczak household, making the transition permanent was more complicated than just signing a few forms in front of a judge. The issue of parental rights lingered. Barbara Valdez was in prison and unable to care for Ronald and me. And though our birth father Oscar did not want to give us up completely, several abusive holiday visits with him and his shy, pretty wife Sylvia left him legally out of the picture.

During the first visit, Oscar had locked Ronald in a dark closet to toughen him up, telling him, "Be a man." That would be hard for any three-year-old child to do, even one who wasn't small for his age. Oscar could thank himself for that. Ronald had born prematurely and therefore smaller because Oscar had beat our mother while she was pregnant, inducing her labor too early.

Ronald and I went back to Oscar just one other time, for Easter. Mom and Dad figured that while we were gone to New York, they would take a trip north to Georgia to see family. Mom and Dad had left phone numbers for any possible place they might be while they were away.

A few days into their visit, Mom and Dad got a call from a social worker. "Inez and Ronald are coming home. We're putting them on a flight to Miami with a case worker."

"What happened? Are they okay?" Dad demanded.

"They're fine. Sylvia is not. There was a domestic violence call to the house, and the children are being removed for their safety."

Sylvia, timid Sylvia, had intervened on my brother's behalf. She had dared to say no to Oscar, a decision which didn't end well for her. The sound of her pretty bangles hitting the mahogany floor has stayed with me through the years.

My memories of Oscar are different. I remember someone who treated me like a princess and showered me with gifts. He made me feel prized, special, important, and wanted. It's a standard that went deep. It still affects how I desire men to treat me today.

My adoption left me in a situation that was doubtless better than the situation I had left as the child of people involved in drug culture. It was surely better than the dozens of foster homes I had visited. But I didn't feel like I belonged. Mine was not a happily ever after story; it felt more like the beginning of Cinderella, not the end.

Separation

From the time I entered foster care until right before my adoption, I never saw my birth mother. So, seeing her for the first time in years was a big event. Mom didn't usually take me to court with her, but she did that day. I was probably five or six.

When she entered the courtroom, Barbara Valdez was wearing a prison jumpsuit and handcuffs to court. She was tall. You could tell she had just been crying, and she had curly brown Cuban hair, which meant that the curls were bushy, loose ringlets. My hair is similar, only now I straighten it to loosen the curl. She was curvaceous with a small waist, the typically attractive figure of a Latin woman.

I sat on a wooden bench between my social worker and my adopted mother while I looked at this stranger who was also my mother. My birth mother was a beautiful woman. But the handcuffs she wore bothered me. I couldn't stand to see them. This woman didn't look dangerous, but here she was restrained.

"Why she got on an orange jumpsuit? Why they got her hands in those things?" I asked Mom, nodding to my birth mother.

What was she supposed to say? There are few acceptable, age-appropriate ways to discuss things like drugs and prostitution with a child. The social worker interrupted.

"She stole a pack of gum," the case worker answered.

Holy smokes! I was terrified. For years, I took the belief with me that you could go to prison in handcuffs for any little offense.

At the end of the court appearance, Barbara Valdez went back to prison, and I went home with Mom. I didn't see my birth mother again for a while. My adopted mom did, though.

Barbara Valdez was brought one day to a room alone with Mom to discuss parental rights. My birth mother knew that she couldn't care for Ronald and me then. Even after she got out of prison, she didn't know what she would do for honest work. She had no money and no family close by. Oscar had abandoned her. She was alone, poor, and marked by her prison stay. But her heart was still full of us.

"If I could see them sometimes, even once a year, I would sign," she said.

"Done," Mom answered.

She was as good as her word. While we lived in Miami, she did take us by the prison a few times to see my birth mother. These visits were short, and I don't remember them. Too much time had passed for Ronald and me to feel a motherly connection to Barbara Valdez. We didn't know how to love her, and she didn't know how to make up for giving us away.

For the second major meeting with my birth mom, my parents used a big van to take us to Tallahassee. I remember it being a hot, sweaty, and long ride from Miami. The saving grace was that we got to have McDonalds, which made it feel like a field trip.

My brother and I were a little confused when Mom and Dad told us we were going to visit Barbara Valdez. We both thought: "What for? I thought we just got adopted." This visit was part of the open adoption agreement. She was allowed to see us if she stayed clean and out of trouble.

When our van finally stopped in front of her house, Ronald and I looked around in confusion and dismay at the host of similar looking squat, brick houses situated in common rows. Our Miami home was a one-level ranch-style brown house, but it was cheerful and well-kept. It had a wide lawn where my siblings and I could play. This neighborhood didn't look or feel like home. It felt dirty and unsafe.

Ronald and I timidly entered with Mom and Dad when our birth mother answered the door. I could tell that Barbara Valdez had done her best to clean up. She had gotten little trinkets to make the place look presentable.

But there was only so much you could do to dress up the projects in Tallahassee. Because I was used to my adopted home, I immediately judged this tiny house. It looked like a square box, with the living room and kitchen close to each other. I smelled something burnt in the air.

My birth mother herself had changed physically. She was so overweight that her face looked distorted to me. The black eyeliner underneath her eyes made her seem unfamiliar, not like the pretty, curvy mother in my memory.

She gave us small gifts, coloring books and crayons, and tried to speak to us. Looking back now, I feel so sorry and uncomfortable thinking of her trying to navigate a conversation with Ronald and me through an interpreter. She asked me repeatedly in broken English about how I was doing in school and what grade I was in. I kept thinking: "My real mother would know."

I felt annoyed, and my brother completely checked out by concentrating on coloring in the coloring book she had given him. Ronald didn't ever look up at her. He just kept coloring. I tried to do the same to let the time run out on our visit, but I was torn between being polite and wanting to be somewhere else.

When Ronald and I said goodbye to Barbara Valdez that afternoon, the separation that began when she walked away from us was complete. I never saw Barbara Valdez again after that visit because she relapsed and was sent back to jail. She lost all parental rights.

It was as if after that meeting, she self-destructed. Perhaps, without anyone to counsel her, she felt defeated and robbed of her opportunity to be the kind of mother who would see and feel something other than disappointment from her kids. Without us, she had little reason to try.

Only now, as a mother, can I connect to her feelings of failure. She had really tried during that Tallahassee visit to connect to Ronald and me. But after so much time and so much trauma, there was nothing she could do to rewrite the past and make us look at her the same way we had as trusting, unwounded babies.

This separation was a tragedy on both sides. I had buried the pain of missing her so deeply that I couldn't understand it. And though our distance was largely not her fault, she was powerless to erase it. I would not fully understand her American horror story until I graduated from college.

Erasure

My formal adoption came with a name change. Mom and Dad changed the names of all the children they adopted, both to claim them as theirs and to impart some special meaning. My name became Inez Marie Sobczak. Mom changed my middle name to honor her mother and the Virgin Mary. This was a name bestowed in love as an homage to her faith.

But when I realized the change later, it didn't feel that way. I felt that something had been taken from me, some part of my Cuban heritage. Inez Marie could be any white girl. Inez Esperanza was definitely Latina. I can understand Mom's reasoning now, but then, it felt like a mark of disapproval of who I was at an essential level.

There was another breach of my Cuban heritage that I didn't feel until after it happened, and that was the move north to Virginia. I was growing up in Miami in the late eighties, when Nancy Reagan was encouraging everyone to just say no to drugs and a significant portion of the population where I lived was telling Nancy, "No thanks."

Drug-fueled violence and gang activity were making Miami a more and more dangerous place to live. Child abductions were becoming common news items. The city didn't feel like the place my parents remembered from their own childhoods anymore. How could they let their kids run around outside all day without panicking that some human trafficker would snatch them and sell them? How could they even let us play in our own front yard?

One day, Dad walked into work and asked for a transfer. The UVA Medical Center needed him, and Dad said, "That sounds perfect." He discussed it with Mom and put the house on the market. It sold in time for all of us to make the move together to Waynesboro, Virginia.

So, they had a farewell party with a cake from a Cuban bakery—the last cake like that one that I would eat for a long time. I didn't realize when I was saying goodbye to neighbors and church members and school friends—many of them Cuban—that I was also saying goodbye to the culture of my birth. I was exchanging tostones and medianoches for fries and burgers. I was exchanging jazz from open house windows for country and western from the lowered windows of pickup trucks. And boy, was I unprepared for that change!

As far as I was concerned, this was a grand adventure. During this move, for the first time in my life, a family was coming with me when I changed locations. Yes, I had to make new friends at school and church, but I would not at the same time have to figure out where I fit in a new family dynamic and rush to be the most useful, orderly, appealing kid in the house. I was excited.

My eighth birthday fell during the move, and we stopped by a Denny's to order a big birthday meal and a fabulous, sloppy ice cream sundae. I thought it was the best birthday in the world. Even to this day, I get a little travel antsy around my birthday. I'd rather be on the go than stay at home when it's time to celebrate.

When we arrived in Waynesboro, we loved our house. It was three stories, including the basement, with plenty of rooms for all of us. We all liked the powder blue siding, the neighborhood full of other kids, and the green everywhere in a yard where we were encouraged to go play.

I hit my stride as a ringleader of the outside games, someone who was always ready to play tag or jump rope or ride bikes anywhere at all. My energy was a valuable commodity here. With this move, I exchanged a large, private religious school where many of my teachers were nuns for a small, rural public school where my classmates were my neighbors and playmates. That was a good situation for me.

However, I was subtly different from these classmates. In a school where the division fell between Black and white children, I was brown enough not to fit in either category. Among a room full of Baptist, Presbyterian, Methodist, and Church of Christ children, I was the lone Catholic. People liked me, but I didn't belong anywhere for sure.

Part of this erasure happened even before my adoption. Being placed with non-Latin families meant that I lost the Spanish language. And after our move, I no longer heard Spanish in the streets. I soon forgot what little I had known. Forgetting my Cuban heritage and language left me unable to communicate with my birth mother on the occasions when she reached out to me.

My story shows one of the reasons transracial adoption support groups are so important. They are on the rise because people in mainstream culture have raised children of different ethnicities without understanding or feeling the need to keep them connected to the culture to which they belonged. Those of us who came from those backgrounds are voicing the need for change.

This realization does not mean that I am ungrateful for the love and care my parents gave me. I know it's easy to look back and say, "You did it wrong," when they did the best they knew. I must extend grace to them, just as I do to my birth mother and to myself.

However, that feeling of being other, of not fitting in, became foundational to my life. Because I didn't know who I was and where I came from, I had to change myself to be like the people around me. Erasure of my heritage set me up for some years of feeling lost. Being Cuban became something I would have to discover when I grew old enough to choose my own way.

INFLUENCES

That early childhood trauma didn't break me. And my later childhood brought more truths, lessons, and blessings from the people that surrounded me. Examining memories from this time brings me clarity on how I receive love and approval.

Childhood is a rich ground for you to explore. As you hear my stories, think about the events that shaped you and changed you. But also remember who added to your life, who protected you, and who showed you who you were in a powerful way.

Church

One event that underscored for me the importance of being Catholic was my first communion, which happened when I was in second grade. In preparation, I had taken classes on the meaning of the faith. Mom and I had shopped for a beautiful, lace-trimmed white satin dress. It was the most beautiful thing I had ever worn. I looked like a tiny bride doll, and I felt like a princess.

When the day came, I rode in our car to the church feeling the solemnity of the occasion. In a room off the sanctuary, I met the other children who were taking their first communion. Other girls in fancy white dresses lined up with me, and beside us boys in grey or black suits fidgeted, spinning on the slick soles of their shiny shoes when no one was looking.

We were marched to the vestibule in front of the closed doors, where we waited a second time. Then a teacher opened the door, and there was the sanctuary. I walked in line to the priest, took the wafer and the wine, and bowed my head with sincere devotion.

As I participated in this ceremony, I felt a deep desire within me to be good. I'd always felt it. It was the reason I was so eager to clean that I put away Meredith's dolls before she was finished playing with them. It was the reason I would go over to my friends' houses and help them clean their rooms. I wanted to be good. And bowing my head while wearing that gown of shining white, I felt that I was good, through and through. I never wanted that feeling to go away.

When the ceremony was over, the other children in my class and I received gifts from the congregation. Then my family came home, and I had a party there with a cake and more presents. I felt like my birthday had come twice that year. Aunt Leslie and Uncle Eddie had flown up from Florida to see me. I felt so loved and celebrated. My mother had my portrait made in that beautiful white dress, just as she had done for Meredith.

That kind of celebration and ceremony was one of the highlights of being raised Catholic. Another was the fact that there was a center to my moral universe. I never had to wonder what was right or wrong because I knew. In a way, the certainty was reassuring to me.

Not long after that beautiful ceremony, though, I had another tangible reminder of the reality of my parents' faith. Social Services called with the news that there was a baby who needed care—a baby with two older brothers. I think my mom lost her heart to them when the case worker told her they looked like little Dutch boys, like her. My parents agreed to take the boys, and immediately our family went from five people to eight people.

It was an adjustment for us kids, at least for Ronald and me. We had kind of assumed that we completed the Sobczak family, and we liked the relationship the five of us shared. To add so many children at once felt unnecessary to us. Weren't we enough?

But Meredith didn't feel that way. Just like Mom, Meredith was excited to welcome more children. She felt about them the same way she had felt about Ronald and me when we arrived.

Mom and Dad weren't done, either. When I was in middle school, they adopted another brother and sister. When they arrived, we went from being a family of eight to being a family of ten. Life in such a big family was sometimes chaotic, usually loud, and never boring. Of course, money never went as far as it would have if Mom and Dad had stuck with their first child and never welcomed any others. But that was not what Mom and Dad wanted.

What they wanted was to live their faith in a practical way. Making a difference in the lives of children at risk was the way they chose to do that. No number of vacations and no amount of luxury could ever be worth more than making their kids part of their family. There was no contest. They would, and did, pick the kids every time.

Money wasn't the only thing that had to stretch. Patience and goodwill had to stretch, too, and not just from our parents to us. All the siblings had to draw on that patience and tolerance with each other, too. Sometimes that was easier than others. There were a lot of different personalities under one roof.

You really had to work hard to stand out in a big family, too. I added to Mrs. Brown's lessons about cleanliness. Now I learned that being a great student would win me attention.

Overall, the faith my parents taught me added a great deal to my life. But I began to see as I grew older the problems it caused as well. The same church which taught God's perfect love also insinuated a distrust of non-white, non-mainstream culture. I felt distrusted and discounted in childhood in part because conservative religious culture distrusted and discounted brown people.

Part of my work as an adult now is untangling the harmful ideas in religion from the helpful ones. I discern where I can accept truth and where people made mistakes. And the rock-bottom truth I take from this work is that God loves me utterly and unconditionally. Despite the ways human beings sometimes failed, I can trust and know that God is good, and he is crazy about me.

Purity

After I came to join the Sobczak family, my childhood was as normal as any adoptee could have, for the most part. Despite the early trauma of separation from my birth mother and being shuffled around the foster care system, I was finding my way. Things were not perfect. But they felt manageable and even hopeful.

Then one day I suffered a loss that broke me in a way I find hard to explain.

I wonder what started the train of thought in Mom's mind about my inner sinfulness. Maybe it was seeing my birth mother and me together for the last time when I was seven, before our move out of state. Maybe it was some deeply ingrained thoughts and beliefs. Maybe it was a remark from a teacher or someone at church about my outgoing, bubbly, talkative nature.

Whatever it was, something happened to convince my mother that I needed a medical checkup to prove my virginity.

At eleven years old, I had little knowledge about the facts of life and absolutely zero experience. No one had ever touched me inappropriately, which was a miracle considering the number of foster homes I'd had as a small child. And most importantly, my mind and heart were not engaged in the kind of preoccupation with boys and sex that would have prompted such a doctor's visit.

In many ways, I was still the little girl in the spotless white first communion dress. I was the innocent child who wanted to be good and please God and her family. I couldn't have imagined the kind of activity that led to pregnancy. I was as holy and stainless before that visit as Mom could have wished me to be.

No one told me what was going to happen, and no one explained to me what was going on or why. I went into the doctor's office with normal expectations of what usually went on in those rooms. But then I was told to remove my clothing and my underclothing and replace them with a flimsy paper gown. That felt wrong, but being a good girl, I obeyed. Had I known why I was exposed, I would have run instead.

I guess my parents thought the less I knew, the better. Later I learned why I had been undressed and prodded in that way. The exam felt like a violation and a punishment. It was certainly a humiliation.

Beyond that, I felt unsafe. This kind of shame and hurt felt like something my parents should have shielded me from experiencing. The fact that they did not protect me from it was another kind of brokenness.

And it sent the message to me loud and clear that Mom did not approve of me, trust me, or like me that much. She thought that I was just like my birth mother, and she expected one day to see me in handcuffs on my way to prison, just like Barbara Valdez. Just like so many of the people who looked like me. Brown. Other. Foreign.

I was certainly and medically a virgin when I entered that doctor's office. All I can tell you is that I didn't feel like one when I left. A world had been opened to me that frightened me, embarrassed me, and made me dislike my physical body in a way I had never thought I would.

However, I didn't show this change in bad behavior or bad grades. Outwardly, I was the same Inez—active, friendly, ambitious, and responsible. But inside, I started to think of myself differently. I felt a basic physical discomfort like my skin crawling whenever I remembered that appointment. I was sure that it showed for others to see.

Looking back on this event, I know that my parents wanted the best for me; they intended to give me a good life. They would not have hurt me knowingly. Their hearts were in the right place. Their actions did not stem from cruelty, but they felt cruel.

Their decision didn't happen in a vacuum, either. There was a whole conversation in the church and in the nation while I was growing up about race and about sex that filtered down into the decision that put me in that exam room. Political and religious ideas don't stay in the realm of thought. Ideas make people do things.

I'm sure I'm not the only one who suffered from mainstream assumptions about minority races. I know for a fact that I'm not the only one who suffered negative effects from purity culture—a culture that distilled a woman's worth down to one fact about her. I tell this story now in part to assure you, my friends reading this book, that you are more than the hurts you suffered.

You are more than the wrong assumptions people make about you. You are more than the tacky jokes and tasteless comments you overhear. You are more than your sexual experiences or your sexual wounds. You are more than the pain you suffered because your parents didn't know how to protect you.

You are the person God sees: worthy, special, precious, and enough just as you are.

Mother

The first time I met my adopted mother, I remember asking her, "Why don't you have gold teeth?" I thought all mothers had gold teeth like Mrs. Brown. But that question was the wrong one to ask.

Maybe I picked up on some facial cues that my new Mom didn't receive that question well. Remember, I was four, and a veteran of more than two dozen home transfers. I needed some love and assurance from this new parent. Sitting there on my adopted mother's lap, I said: "I love you, Mama."

How would you respond to those words from a small child? I expected that I would get something kind, "I love you, too," or even, "Oh, how sweet!"

The response I remember and the one she still talks about to her sisters is her saying: "I got your number." Her first words to me, "I got your number," summed me up as a manipulative child, someone she had to watch with suspicion.

Right after those words, she also said, "I'm gonna show her," words which established us as adversaries. From the moment I came into the house, in her mind, I was Mom's opponent. I did not make that choice. She did.

My birth mother, poor and battling addiction, presented one kind of danger; my birth father, abusive and shady, presented another. Though they loved me, they weren't good for me. Physical distance from them was necessary.

At my new home, I traded those dangers for physical safety. But I lost love and acceptance. My new Mom fed, sheltered, and clothed my body, and she taught and guided my mind. My heart, though, was starved. From the beginning, I had a mother who couldn't accept me.

I struggled to fit in. Granted, it was Miami, and I was outside in the sun playing a lot and tanning while I did. But I was darker than the rest of the family, darker even than Ronald. While Ronald had learned a slight Spanish accent from his foster parents, I had picked up some straight-up ghetto sass from mine—accent and vocabulary. Mom found Ronald's speech charming and mine worrisome.

Part of the reason was that my mom was sincerely devout. She wanted a house full of kids who loved God and did their best to please him. I didn't fit her picture.

My natural, boundless energy was a little too much for her, too. She can remember my running into the house so fast that I hit the corner of the wall with my head, making a thunk like a ripe watermelon. There was blood everywhere, and Mom and Dad had to pack up all the kids and take me to the emergency room. That was on her birthday. Yikes.

Meredith remembers another instance of my restless athletic drive. I had just arrived, and Mom and Dad hadn't had time to get me a bed. I slept on a cot next to Meredith's bed, which was invitingly fluffy and bouncy. I climbed up on it and jumped up and down and up and down and then up and forward, hitting my head on the ceiling fan and falling to the floor, stunned. I could not be stopped.

Growing up, the division between Mom and me deepened. Perhaps it was inevitable. We are just very different people. She was quiet and withdrawn; I was loud and outgoing. She focused on charity and homemaking. I focused on exercise and my friends. I knew early on the things that were important to Mom. Those were not the things that were the most important to me.

As I grew older, my parents put me into Catholic school, which was difficult. I was always being singled out there for wearing my skirt short, showing my cleavage, or some other problem they had with my uniform. Because I was built like a Latin woman, my uniform was not going to look the same on me as it did on my white counterparts. There was little I could do practically to conform the way the teachers and administrators wanted me to look.

The administration wasn't my only problem. Apart from a few close friends, the other girls made my life difficult. They picked on my hair, my face, my body, and my personality, backing me into a corner where I had to fight to survive. Those confrontations often ended in fights, and I got into trouble at school for those fights.

That trouble followed me home. Mom just saw that I was getting into trouble. If I ended up in the principal's office, it must be my fault. I must have done something to provoke the other girls. It must have looked to her like I was just fulfilling her expectations, legitimizing her fears of who I would become. A troublemaker with brown skin had produced me, and the apple had not fallen far from the tree.

Mom was angry that switching schools had not solved her problem with me. Our tension boiled over sometimes to the point where I had to fight her physically the same way I had to fight the girls at school who bullied me. These physical altercations resulted either in her telling me to leave her house or in me escaping to my friend Jamie's house or eventually to my boyfriend's house.

I know I am not alone. Many women have issues with their mothers. Motherhood is hard, even when that child comes from your body and your genes. And the mistakes mothers make are often especially deep and wounding because we need them so much.

We also can't forget that mothers are daughters, too. Their mistakes likely flow from ways they weren't mothered well when they were children. We could take this pattern back to Eve, who let her children down by losing a perfect home and placing them in danger out in the world. It is useful only in a limited way to keep looking back.

What is more useful is to look at ourselves now, in the ways we nurture the people around us. We can choose to notice the mothering we didn't get and find ways to bring others the support and comfort we didn't receive. We can turn this place of hurt into a place of power. Whatever motherhood looks like in our lives, we can redeem it.

We can do this because motherhood is a place of creativity. We can all choose to create love. We can all choose to create belonging. We can change the story now, so that we hand the next generation a much better one.

Father

The parent who was close to me was Dad. Dad, a scientist as well as a man of faith, believed in the power of genetics and peer-reviewed studies and explained things that way. He thought it was genuinely interesting having kids from so many birth families in the same adopted family. That was Dad, positive, curious, and intellectual.

I didn't feel a sense of disapproval from Dad. I felt that he was optimistic about me, and I knew that he liked having me around. He put me and Ronald into soccer, and he coached our team. I can still hear his voice cheering me on from the sidelines.

For a kid like me who was always being reminded to slow down and be quiet, sports were a literal salvation. Out on the field, I was not just allowed but encouraged to run as fast as I could. No one cared if I yelled across the field to a teammate or turned a cartwheel on the grass to show some happiness. I developed an attachment to team movement that would benefit me the rest of my life. I'm grateful to Dad for seeing that quality in me and doing something to foster it.

As I grew older, I saw my father's love for me in his constant acceptance and support. Even when I disappointed him, I knew that he loved me. He might not like my actions, but he liked who I was as a person.

He didn't shy away from telling me the truth about my heritage. To help me avoid pitfalls, he told me that relationships would be hard for me and that my best way forward in life was to read and learn everything I could. I listened to him because I knew he cared.

When I got into trouble with Mom, my father would often come to my defense, which would result in their fighting behind closed doors about me. Dad was the one who told me I was allowed home when Mom's anger forced me out of the house. I felt bad about that part. Truly, I had no desire to cause trouble in my family. But I was glad I had at least one parent willing to fight for me instead of against me.

Around the time I switched schools, Dad started working with Ronald and me on a soap box derby entry. I loved spending time with Dad and handling those tools. It was exciting to see something sturdy and useful take shape under my hands.

While Ronald viewed the derby as a kind of fun project that he would do because Dad was excited about it, I viewed it as a big opportunity. Not only would I build the best and fastest racer in town, but I would also use the chassis to make a statement to the whole city.

Along the side of my racer, I printed "Girls Can, Too!" a daringly feminist statement for that community at that time, and I got sponsors for my racer—neighbors, women from church, and shop owners. Anyone looking at my car would think that I had confidence for miles. But as bold as those words were, they didn't express how I felt about myself. I felt insecure and unlovable in a lot of ways.

So, when I pulled up to the starting line on the day of the derby, I was eager to race. I just didn't think I deserved to win. I pushed those feelings aside during the first rounds and made it to the finals. As fast as I was on the soccer field, I was faster on pavement with well-greased wheels under me. I put my heart into the final length, easily pulling into the front of the pack.

Then, I couldn't tell you exactly what happened. It seemed to happen without any conscious thought. It was like something in my body was saying, "No. You don't belong. This is not for you." And I ran off the course to the side.

Dad was understanding and kind. He was sincerely proud of how far I had made it in the derby, and he assumed I just panicked or made a mistake. He hugged me and told me I'd done a good job.

How could I tell him that I hadn't done a good job? How could I tell him that I had pushed that win away from me because I didn't deserve it? Those feelings didn't make any sense to me; I couldn't even consciously acknowledge them. There was no way I could have explained them to him at the time and made him understand that I didn't deserve his sympathy and encouragement. It would take me a long time to understand those feelings in myself. It would take other times when I sabotaged myself as an adult in more disastrous ways. But all those failures came from the same core trauma: the belief that I wasn't good.

Looking back on this memory, I see two sides of this race. The first, the loss, shows me how wounded I was deep inside. I had brought all the rejection and judgement I felt deep inside me to a place where it felt like it was coming from me. At the time, I couldn't separate my birth mother abandoning me and my adopted mom disliking me from how I felt about myself.

The other side is what happened after the loss. The way Dad praised me and comforted me assured me that he accepted and loved me. I can see now, too, that Dad's reaction prepared me to accept the reality of a heavenly father who could love me and accept me completely, even when I felt that I had messed up too badly to deserve it.

We can all connect with some good things in our lives by thinking about the people who championed us. Someone in our childhoods could look at us with excitement and fondness and make us feel like we were okay. Someone took our side and protected us. Embracing those memories can give us a strong place to start with healing and recovery.

For us to succeed at making real changes, we need to believe that we're worth the effort. We need to believe that someone out there knows we can do it, because if that person knows it, we can adopt that certainty for ourselves. Maybe what you need right now is to hear a familiar voice from the sidelines yelling your name with pride, watching you fly forward with the message that you can, too.

Friends

When I reached middle school and started attending a public school that was much larger than my small, rural elementary school for the first time, kids from the country club side of Waynesboro were mixing with kids from the lower middle-class side. I had been popular with the kids who knew me from my younger years, and so I entered this new environment with a reputation as fun, energetic, and interesting.

In middle school, being highly visible is not always a good thing. Sure, people want to be your friend—some people. Other people want to knock you off your pedestal.

And the fact that middle school and high school are so tribal didn't help me, either. The Black and white divide that I'd first noticed when I moved to Waynesboro widened when you added puppy love into the mix. Usually, white girls competed for the white boys, while Black girls competed for the Black boys. Nobody dreamed of interracial mixing in central Virginia, at least not where I was.

So, what was a brown girl in a white family to do? I seemed like a threat to the girls in both potential dating pools. At the same time, I seemed a little out of bounds for both white boys and Black boys. I didn't belong in the Jenga tower of their interpersonal relationships. I could bring the whole thing crashing down.

The question of whether I was white or Black (Latina was unknown in that area; I might as well have said I was a Martian) resolved itself when my hormones got to work. I developed the curves of a brown woman, which were close enough to the curves of a Black woman to declare my allegiance for me. Coupled with my brown eyes and brown curls, I had little chance of passing for a Jennifer or a Jessica.

Fortunately, I found loyal friends in Jamie and Debra, two Black girls who took me in and treated me like family. They and their mothers guided me through the winding maze of my teen years. They knew very well how to manage frizzy, voluminous locks and how to dress the larger cup sizes and hip sizes that my Latin genes had bestowed on me.

Jamie came from a family of hardworking entrepreneurs who owned a restaurant. Debra's father was a minister, and he and her mother expected her to keep her grades and her moral standards high. Their families were the opposite of the lawless people who had brought me into the world, and I imagine that Mom breathed a cautious sigh of relief when I formed friendships with such upstanding people.

I just liked Jamie and Debra because they were fun to hang around, loyal to a fault, and generous with their acceptance and affection. Jamie's mom knew what ice cream I liked (tin roof) and bought it at the store for me when she shopped for groceries for her family. Debra's mom liked me so much that she would side with me over Debra if we disagreed.

Friendship with Jamie and Debra made life easier for me at school, too. I was naturally friendly and willing to approach everyone with no judgement. But I soon learned that not everyone approached me the same way. Girls picked fights with me that I didn't want and never invited. If I had not had Jamie and Debra there to take up for me and stand beside me, I would have come off much worse in those fights.

Jamie told me that the other girls were just jealous of me. I couldn't understand or accept her words deep down. If it was jealousy that sparked the fights, it didn't feel that way. It felt like hatred and rejection, unreasoning and fierce. There was no way to stop the attacks, and there was no way to explain them adequately at home.

When Dad and Mom decided together that public school wasn't working out for me, I left the middle school where Jamie and Debra went and started attending a Catholic school nearby. I kept up my friendship with the girls, though. Nothing was going to separate me from my true and loyal friends. Debra and Jamie were constants in my life while I struggled to find out who I was and where I fit in. It didn't matter to them that I didn't look like them or worship where they did or that my parents had chosen me, not birthed me. I was family to them, and they were sisters to me.

Jamie and Debra taught me that friendship is all about acceptance, loyalty, love, and forgiveness. Even today, when we don't see each other as much, I know that our bond is still intact. Friendship like theirs is forever.

Our friends are so important to us not only because they provide us with love and companionship but also because they show us who we are. We become like the people we choose to have around us. That's why it's so important to choose people who can encourage us to become better, to keep growing, and to make healthy decisions.

We look around at our friend group, and we can see both the past and the future. Yes, we can see our memories together and the places we came from. At the same time, we can see our pursuits, our dreams, and our habits.

Look very carefully at what your friends are showing you about yourself. Do you like what you see?

Mentors

Other adults entered my life as I grew and gave me the love and approval that I needed. I didn't have to look far for most of these people. Some of them, like Dad, were in my family.

Dad's mother loved me in very practical ways, always including me whenever I was around. Grandma Sobczak would visit for long stretches of time, especially after her husband passed away. My dad didn't like for her to be alone.

I can remember going to church with her and lighting candles to pray for people we loved. For her, faith was a very tender thing, a way to send her caring heart out into the world and the universe. Being with her there helped me reclaim some of that feeling of holiness and goodness I had felt when I was a small child taking my first communion.

But she was very independent. If she missed playing cards with her friends, she would tell Dad, "I'm going home." She didn't ask him; she just went. I liked her for that spunk.

Another person I was sure liked me was my Aunt Leslie. She sent me cards for every single birthday and went out of her way to make Christmas special for me and my siblings. Without kids of her own, she looked on her sister's big family as an opportunity to love us all in her generous way. She provided some motherly love, affection, and approval that I needed.

I remember her looking into my eyes with genuine care and interest. I felt that I could talk to her and that she wanted to hear what I had to say. She thought I was beautiful and liked my big brown eyes, and she told me so. Her warmth went straight to my heart.

She also provided me with a visual of another way to be a woman. Where Mom was home-centered and more introverted, Aunt Leslie devoted time to her career and to fitness. I saw that because she made those choices, she was able to afford gifts and vacations that my parents just couldn't buy.

Not that she was materialistic—she and her firefighter husband were both caring, giving people. But I found value in being able to make other people happy with presents, just like she did. That was something I wanted to do someday. And I loved how she looked so put-together and elegant whenever I saw her. It was how I wanted to appear when I grew up.

Aunt Leslie's example in fitness motivated me early on. I can remember her going out for a morning jog while she was on a visit. Intrigued, I asked her, "Can I come with you?"

"Sure," she smiled. "We'll run together."

That was a really happy memory for me, keeping up with Aunt Leslie. I loved the sensation of running. I also loved the feeling of being wanted and included. I wanted more of both those things.

One place I found them was Girl Scouts. Being a Scout—learning skills and earning badges—made me happy. I've always been an achiever! I loved being with other girls my age and going on outings like camping trips and cookie sales. It was such a positive place for me that I stayed in till my teen years and earned my gold award.

I also loved my Scout leader, Barbara Powell. Miss Powell, an older lady who knew everything in the guidebook, was unafraid to tell the girls in her troop when we stepped out of line. But she liked us and loved being around us. Her corrections never stung, and I never feared that she would think less of me.

She could, and did, catch me sneaking cookies in the church kitchen, talking out of turn, and wandering off into the woods to explore with a friend or two. She was someone who could tell me in one breath to put the cookies down and get back to the group and in the next breath tell me that I was her pride and joy and that she was so proud of me. That balance, rare and precious, meant everything to me.

Miss Powell made the time to take our troop to Virginia Beach or on sleepovers to the aquarium. She put the effort into helping us sell our last few boxes of cookies when sale time was closing. She never gave up on us. A lot of us were girls that society had already written off. Not her. I still have a picture of her holding me as I received my gold award. She was a superhero to me.

Thank goodness I had these mentors. As a child who had lost and suffered a lot in my early years, I needed love and affirmation. In Grandma Sobczak, Aunt Leslie, and Miss Powell, I found the encouragement I craved.

Fitness

One extremely good thing that happened in my life as a teenager was my discovery of fitness in a more solid and empowered way. I had left organized sports behind when I left my public middle school, and I missed being active that way. Fortunately, Dad saw that, too.

The basement was kind of his domain. He kept some tools there for repair projects and some fun things like building those soap box derby racers. He also kept workout equipment. I would see him disappear down the basement stairs, and then I would hear Pink Floyd on the record player.

After I changed schools, I started following Dad down the basement stairs and doing what he did. I jumped rope. I lifted weights. I did calisthenics. And I loved it!

Fitness became such an important part of my life that I wanted access to more of it than I could find in the basement.

So, I joined the YMCA in town, just me alone. I made a solid move to get something I wanted and needed.

One day, I heard music and laughter as I passed by a classroom of women doing step classes. I was mesmerized. The music was loud and fun, and all the ladies looked like they were having a great time. I wanted in!

Now if you've ever been to a step class, you know that you start toward the back of the room while you're learning the moves, and then you move upward as you get better. This habit makes sense, because that way the people in the back who are learning have people in front to watch. Also, the new learners don't have to worry about embarrassing themselves where everyone can see. Win-win.

My little fifteen-year-old self didn't bother with the way things were done, though. I caught on to the movement fast and went straight to the front of the room. There was a move called "around the world" that made me feel like a superhero every time I hit it! I was hooked.

Luckily, the women there embraced me and took my boldness as just the natural enthusiasm and love of fun that it was. In that room, I felt something shift in my perception of the way the world worked the same way I had when Aunt Leslie had invited me on her jog.

Exercising like this was something women did together. They gossiped and laughed and cheered each other on. They made friends. And they had a wonderful time.

At home, I hadn't seen this part of life because it wasn't something Mom valued. So, stumbling on that step class felt like a secret treasure. It felt like I knew something even she didn't know.

The instructor, Jenny Hasshagen with American Fitness Federation Association, saw some potential in me and invited me to train as an instructor with her organization. I gladly took those classes and got my certification. At fifteen, I started leading women in fitness classes. Looking back, I see that I naturally gravitated toward doing what I now know is my calling in life: helping other people be their best.

And I loved teaching fitness classes. First, that meant that I was doing a fitness class, which was one of my favorite things. It also meant that I was out of the house, away from the tension with Mom and the pressure to conform. And as a bonus, I got paid. But I really think I would have done those classes for free because I loved them so much. In fact, Jamie complained sometimes that I never wanted to do anything fun anymore. All I wanted to do was go to the gym.

That wasn't entirely true; I was making time for my grades and my friends. But it was true that I had found a true love and a lifelong passion. In fitness, I had found a practice that made use of my natural energy and positivity. Helping other people discover it was a key that unlocked my purpose and potential.

A lot of us forget who we are in the pressure to meet other people's expectations. We love or admire or respect or even fear the people with authority in our lives, whether those are older leaders like parents and teachers or whether they're peers we've given the right to speak into our lives. Then, instead of growing into our unique abilities and preferences, we compromise. We do what sounds reasonable or practical instead of what we love.

A good practice is to think about what brought us true joy as children. We can recall what made us laugh out loud, what we spent hours doing—so absorbed that we didn't notice the time passing. When we hold those memories in front of us, we can ask ourselves how we can bring those first loves into our adult lives.

We all deserve to spend our time doing what makes us feel powerful, known, and alive. Childhood can be the perfect place to help us understand exactly what that is.

TRIALS

As I grew older and understood more about the world, I started to view my early life differently. And my widening independence meant that I could make choices for myself, choices that didn't always work out for me. The events of these years led to patterns of behavior that would lead me to the lowest points of my life.

While you read these stories, think about your own growing pains. Think about the trials that shaped you, whether they arose from your actions or someone else's. How might they still be affecting you today?

Attack

Like any young teenage girl, I was susceptible to the attentions of an older boy who thought I was cute. His name was Beef. Now, I laugh out loud at how I could ever have thought that was a cool nickname. Beef. Right?

I agreed for him to come to pick me up and then lied to my parents about where I was going. I said I was going over to Jamie's house, but I arranged to meet Beef at Jamie's work instead. I mean, I was 14, and an older guy liked me. I wasn't going to give my parents the chance to stop me from dating him.

Meredith had noticed me flirting with Beef, who was a local drug dealer. She told Mom and Dad that I was drawing the attention of an older guy. She didn't know him well, but she looked at the age difference between us and got scared. Beef was around her age, and she was three years older than I was. I'm sure one or both of my parents warned me about messing around with older guys. But I'm equally sure that the lecture they delivered got lost in a lot of other ones that I was tuning out.

So, when this yellow Cadillac pulled up to Jamie's workplace, I guessed it was Beef. I looked for him inside the car, but I didn't see him. Neither of these guys was Beef. The driver was some other guy named Vincent. The people in the car called him V.

Now, Beef used to sell drugs, and it was not uncommon for him to send people on errands. I figured Beef had sent these guys to pick me up. I just kind of knew not to ask questions because I already had lied to get into this situation.

I wasn't in too deep, I told myself. Beef was not my boyfriend. He was an older boy who liked me and showed me some attention. I was just going to go out with him and have some fun, maybe flirt some more. Maybe he would kiss me.

Doing my best to sound brave, I asked, "Where is Beef?"

Without really looking my way, one of the guys said, "He's on the way."

But these guys in the car were not the guys I was supposed to be with. They took me to a neighboring town, and we stopped at someone's trailer house. There were curtains on the windows that made the small, dim space even dimmer. Someone brought out a bottle, and we all started drinking. There was Mad Dog liquor everywhere, the inexpensive stuff winos drink that tastes like grape juice but is a lethal cocktail. Here's the thing: I didn't drink. Up until that point, I had not drunk anything with alcohol in it except cough syrup when I was sick. Now, I was drinking hard stuff meant to get tough guys drunk fast. And I was a child.

I was scared. Things were not turning out the way I had anticipated. But what could I do? I stayed with these guys I didn't know and did what they were doing because I was too scared to go home after I had lied. Part of me was just praying that I would survive. I didn't feel able to hope for more than that.

I don't really remember what happened next. It has been buried so long. All I do remember is how dark it was in the house. I remember something being really wet, and my head was foggy. I hurt. I asked, "What's going on?" I didn't remember who these guys were. Then I said, "I'm bleeding."

The guy next to me said, "Oh." He just stopped what he was doing.

"What was that?" I asked.

He said, "Oh, it was my fingers."

But it wasn't his finger. Remember, I had endured that vaginal exam. I knew what a finger felt like. This was definitely not the same.

I remember him saying, "I'll give you a moment to clean up." As if he were being some kind of considerate gentleman. The nerve!

By the time I got home, I was blacked out drunk and stumbling. My parents were furious. I couldn't tell them that I had just been given liquor and raped because I felt like the attack was my fault. After all, I had lied.

The next day, Mom and Dad never really talked about my sneaking out and coming home drunk. They let the punishment speak for them. But that incident was always a shadow over my parents' view of me. They became even more determined, more vigilant to do everything they could do as my parents to save me from myself. In return, I never told them about the rape.

If I could go back and talk to the young girl I was, suffering from that rape, I would tell her that what happened was not her fault. Neither was being unable to report it when she was already traumatized, or healing from it imperfectly in the ways that were available to her. She did the best she could with what she had, and I'm proud of her for leading me where I am now.

As children, we sometimes hide what we should tell. We bring blame inside us where it doesn't belong, and we don't let it go. Does this sound familiar to you?

If it does, then practice love and compassion towards the younger you who couldn't deal with the suffering. Write a letter or speak out loud to the child you were. Bring the perspective and strength you have now to that self. It is never too late to offer that love.

Abuse

In some ways, I'm fortunate that my brain and heart protected me by putting all my bad memories and traumas behind a thick, thick wall in my mind. But those memories were still there, even if I couldn't access them. And partly because they were hidden, their power multiplied.

So, I worked hard at what I wanted to focus on: achievement, friendship, and approval. And all the time, the darkness of the memories inside me influenced my decisions. I thought I was making decisions for me, but I was recreating situations that felt familiar.

For instance, I met my first real boyfriend outside Catholic school. We dated for two years. He and I had mutual friends, and I thought he was funny and attractive. He also sold drugs, like many of the people in the less lucky parts of town did to make ends meet. His side hustle meant that he was sometimes around unsavory people doing dangerous things. Through him, I met some of those unsavory people, too.

However, Ryan wasn't just a drug dealer. He was a smart guy who dreamed about a future with meaning and purpose. We used to study together. I wouldn't have been so interested him if he was just some small-town thug. And he respected me.

I was sixteen by this time, and a lot of things had changed for me. I was able to work, and I fully took advantage of that opportunity at the Peebles in town. Work for me meant freedom. With my own money, I could decide things about my appearance that had been out of my reach before. I started getting my hair pressed and my nails done. I bought outfits at Peebles and dressed to the height of nineties fashion.

Money meant that I could drive, now, too, and so I was able to decide where I spent my time and with whom. That was a freedom I'd had to work much harder to exercise before I could drive. It used to mean getting rides or taking long walks. Now it meant grabbing my keys.

I used that little car to express myself, too. My first license plate read CUBANO, a proudly defiant declaration from an English-speaking teenager who wanted desperately to rediscover her identity. It felt good to shout it to the world that way.

Also, dating was available to me in a much safer way. Never again would I have to rely on a boy I didn't know to take me anywhere. I would show up where and when I chose with a ready way of escape if anything didn't feel right.

But things felt right with my boyfriend Ryan, even though they shouldn't have. I told him when we got together that I wasn't going to sleep with him. I had things to do and places to go, and I wasn't going to wind up stuck in Waynesboro with a baby hanging off my hip at seventeen. No way. I was getting out and making something of myself, and I wasn't going to let anything stand in my way—no matter how cute he was.

He completely accepted my boundary and still wanted to go out with me. I felt so special to be valued for more than an avenue to gratification. His agreement meant that I was worth a lot—me, as a person, not just my body. That respect totally won my heart.

It also swayed my resolve. After we had dated for a year, I told him I was losing my virginity to him, as if I was giving him a special gift. Well, I was giving him a special gift. It just wasn't the gift of my virginity. That wasn't mine to give anymore because it had been taken from me.

With that act, I cemented a toxic relationship. What was toxic in our relationship was not our physical intimacy. What was toxic was the physical abuse that I chose to overlook.

I ignored the fact that he hit me sometimes. I was dating a tough guy, after all. I couldn't expect him to be a softie, to change everything that had poured into him while he was growing up. I had to take him as he was. That was love, wasn't it?

That meant that while I was with him, I led a double life. I made straight As at school, worked my heart out at step class, volunteered with the Boys and Girls Club, aced Girl Scouts, and went to church with my huge Catholic family. That was one side.

Then hanging out with Ryan and his friends, exploring my sexuality, taking hard knocks, and remaining silent about the abuse and the dealing—that was another side.

But I felt that I was forced into some kind of duality, because there was no room for me, the Cubano me, the active me, the ambitious me, around Mom. Dad welcomed more of me, though he was wary of my genes and would have been horrified that I knew anyone involved in drugs. After all, hadn't he moved his family away from Miami to keep them away from drug dealers and the criminal element drugs invited into society?

Finally, fate made the decision that I had put off. We were at a party when Ryan laid hands on me. Things got out of hand, and someone called the police. They took Ryan away. That arrest effectively ended our relationship.

As I look back on that relationship now, I can see that it was fortunate for me that an unstoppable outside force ended that relationship. I didn't have the ability at that time in my life to choose my own safety, my own welfare. I needed time and experience to be able to make those decisions for myself.

Looking over our lives to discover our narrow escapes can be really informative for us. We can see dangerous behavior that something else had to stop. Then we can look at the patterns of our behaviors now. What are we doing that won't end well? When we have our answers, we can pump our brakes now, instead of waiting for an inevitable wreck.

Rejection

By the point of Ryan's arrest, Mom and Dad seemed tired of my struggles to figure out who I was and what I wanted. Because I kept landing in situations that cast me in a bad light—in the principal's office because of a fight, coming home bruised and distraught, coming home drunk, getting caught sneaking out—they just couldn't get up any excitement for my triumphs.

The sneaking out happened most memorably with Debra. Though Debra stopped coming to Girl Scouts in high school, she and I spent time at each other's houses a lot. I liked staying over with her upright but tender father, Reverend Freeman, and her warm, encouraging mom. They treated me like their own—even when that meant pulling me back in line.

I will never forget one night when Debra and I sneaked out of her house. I was over to spend the night, and we heard about a party at her aunt's house across town. Because we were sleeping in the basement, we figured that we could leave through the basement window, walk to the party, have a blast, and get back in through the window without Reverend and Mrs. Freeman knowing anything about it.

The first part of our plan worked perfectly. We left the house, giggling and running, and actually enjoyed our nighttime stroll through quiet Waynesboro. Looking at the sleeping houses we passed, we almost felt like we were pulling something over on the whole town. When we got to the party, Debra's family was happy to see us. We got to dance and flirt and joke with everyone there. So far, our risk was paying off.

Our walk home to the Freeman house was a little less fun. We were tired and ready to slip into our sleeping bags. But when we got back, the basement window was locked. That meant that Debra and I had to go to the front door, where we found Reverend Freeman waiting for us. He talked very seriously to Debra and me. We were smart girls and leaders.

Because we had so many natural gifts, we owed it to ourselves and to society to make the most of them.

Disappointing the Freemans felt horrible. I knew that they were very particular about who they allowed to spend time with Debra. They thought highly of me because I prioritized school, came from a religious family, and treated them with respect. And here I had disrespected them in a serious way by deceiving them under their roof.

Shame filled me, and I felt tears in my eyes. The Reverend sent me into one room and Debra into another while he waited for Dad. That was another reason the Freemans accepted me as a friend for Debra. They knew that Mike and Barbara agreed with their standards and would reinforce them at home.

Luckily, the Freemans' brand of religion included a sincere belief in forgiveness. After Debra and I paid for our transgressions, Reverend and Mrs. Freeman restored me to the family circle. They saw past my mistakes to the good in me. I'll always be grateful for that grace.

Contrasting with this grace I saw in my friend's house, my house seemed to be a place where my mistakes and transgressions were never truly forgiven. Instead, they led to a horrible distance between me and my family—especially Mom.

I saw this distance in a painful way at the end of my time in high school. I was named in the top five highest GPAs in the school—and this was a massive school, a gathering point of many school systems in the area. I graduated in a class of

106 seniors. You could mistake my high school for a college campus if you didn't know what it was.

The principal invited my parents to a small ceremony for my name to be announced. I wore my graduation gown and waited for them. But when they arrived, it felt like they were visiting celebrities stopping by for a photo op. They posed with me and offered congratulations. But those words felt like they were coming from strangers who were happy for me only on a surface level. I felt that they didn't truly appreciate or applaud how hard and faithfully I had worked for those grades over four years. And I knew that, in their eyes, this honor didn't make up for the trouble I had caused them.

Part of the reason I knew so is that my parents had attended another ceremony for me recently. Along with several other recipients, I was being honored for my volunteer work with the Boys and Girls Club. I invited my parents with the hope that they would see that in my own way, I was being good. Even if I wasn't the person they wanted me to be, I was doing worthwhile things. But when the ceremony was over and photos were snapped, Mom tossed off a casual remark implying that I had obtained that award because of my body, not my heart.

That remark wounded my soul deeply. I had felt Mom's disapproval of me for years. I had understood that I disappointed her, that I failed to measure up to who she wanted me to be. But that remark told me that she disliked me, that I disgusted her in some way. I felt as if she had slapped my face in front of everyone.

Our distance solidified at my high school graduation. I saw my parents only for pictures. Other than that time, I celebrated the day with my friends. But I felt very alone, very small, and very sad. It was not the day I had anticipated for four years.

Dad was caught in the middle of our tension. He wanted to be a team player with his wife, whom he loved. He was genuinely worried about me because of the choices I was making in dating and friendship. He also loved me and believed in me. And he liked me.

When I was sorting through possibilities for college, Dad helped me decide what I should do and where I should go. I still had the idea in my head that success meant being a doctor or a lawyer. As the daughter of a medical professional, I didn't find healthcare appealing; that left the law. I decided to double-major in philosophy and political science.

Out of the options available to me, I was most drawn to Lynchburg College. The pre-law program was solid, and I had a scholarship. Also, it was over two hours away from Waynesboro. So far away, I wouldn't have to feel Mom's rejection. I didn't want to cut ties with my family permanently, but two and a half hours seemed like a nice buffer.

I was excited to leave for school. In a completely new environment, I would have the chance to make my own reputation. People meeting me would see me just as Inez, not as the adopted kid, the girl from the big family, or the girl who got in trouble a lot. I had no history, nothing dragging me down. I could find acceptance on my own.

Leaving

Before the academic term began my freshman year, I participated in the Student Transition Program, a time of instruction and bonding that the college sponsored to help minority students adjust and succeed. I found a second family in the people who came to STP together. We formed the kind of close, instant bonds that you can only feel when your life is changing completely, and everything feels new.

It was like *Friends*, but with 30 people of color in Virginia. In other words, it was much, much cooler.

Beginning college was wonderful for me. In this larger academic environment, people were more likely to understand what being Cuban meant. At the same time, my race didn't matter as much as my gifts. People appreciated my intellect, as well as how much fun I was at parties and events. Soon I was stepping into a leadership role in college life, planning fundraisers and celebrations. I felt truly alive and connected in that place.

The friendships I formed there meant a lot to me, too, even though I sometimes didn't realize the impact I was having or how other people were taking me. One example is with a roommate, Kathleen, who was feeling insecure about an outfit she had planned. She tried it on for me and asked what I thought in that voice that means, "Please don't let me make a fool of myself in front of everybody. If I look hideous, it is your duty to tell me and save me from myself."

But she looked great, and I told her so. "The key to wearing what you want is confidence. If you look like you belong in those clothes, then you do."

She went out, rocked her fashion choice, and came back after a really good day. That incident passed out of my mind; it was just one of a lot of days with her. But to her, it was a moment when another woman took the opportunity to be kind and lift her up. It stayed with her.

Another moment of encouragement that took root happened with my friend Aaron, a fellow STP member. I sneaked in to watch him play basketball for fun with the guys, and I saw how good he was. Now, Aaron is not a proud person; he's kind and generous and empathetic. So, when I told him how good he was and that he should try out for the school team, at first he dismissed my words as just me being kind. But I insisted, and he listened. And the school basketball team, which he made and where he excelled for years, added a lot to his college career.

But I wasn't Saint Inez at all. I was a lot for some people to handle. Having grown up in a large household with sisters, I was fairly unfamiliar with the concept of private property. We all borrowed each other's stuff at home, and I treated college like home until my friend Emefa pulled me up short.

An only child, Emefa had learned early in childhood to keep her belongings neat, clean, orderly, and private. She was unprepared to encounter hurricane Inez, a force composed in equal parts of enthusiasm, joy, and closeness, with a dash of chaos to shake things up. She kept quiet about her dislike of my borrowing her things until she couldn't hold in her feelings anymore. We fought—she was frustrated while I was offended—and stayed away from one another for a year. But we made up. Her friendship meant so much to me. She was an intelligent, powerful, classy Black woman who gave off strong professional vibes, and I was drawn to her almost immediately, just the way I'd been drawn in middle school to Jamie and Debra.

Luckily, I didn't have to miss my Waynesboro sisters by choice for long. Jamie and Debra both ended up moving to Lynchburg while I was in college. Jamie stayed longer than Debra, who had endured a family tragedy a few years before when her dad, Reverend Freeman, always so dependable and kind, died suddenly.

My friend and her entire family were devastated by the loss, which hit me hard, too. To lose Reverend Freeman felt like losing a father. After she lost her father, Debra and I became less close. After her move to Lynchburg didn't work out as planned, she moved away. We just didn't see each other as much.

But those friends who have been loyal and faithful to you for years are always waiting there for you to reach out. Debra stayed in my life, and she's still in touch. We share something you can't easily replace: a childhood full of memories, including precious memories of her dad.

Fortunately, when I started college, I started it with this soft landing place of having my best friends in town. Though they weren't going to college themselves, they showed up to the parties I planned, and so they got the benefit of some college experiences through me. It worked out well for all of us.

When the first year ended, I went back home to Waynesboro, but I went with a mission. Scholarship or no, I was going to earn as much money as I could make over the summer. I found a job at a factory in town and worked every hour it could give me. When I wasn't working there, I taught fitness classes, a practice I had kept up during college terms, too. I saw my family very little, mostly legitimately because I was so busy. But there was some avoidance there, too. The wounds formed in my teens hadn't healed yet.

When August ended and I returned to Lynchburg, I came back with $60,000 in my bank account. I had worked hard. Now I could focus on studies and college life.

Coping

College life sounds a lot cooler than it was. Now that I look back on it, almost every event followed the same pattern. Get dressed up in some crazy outfit to match a theme or in your flyest fashion to turn some heads, and then follow the sound of loud music to the place. Once there, dance, tease, flirt, talk, laugh, drink, and take a picture. I have so many pictures in my albums that basically say, "We're here, we look amazing, and we're happy."

I drank at these parties, which were mostly on the weekends. I figured that if I had worked hard, I deserved to play hard. But drinking at a party didn't seem problematic to me, mostly because I never drank during the week, when I had to learn and produce work for class. I kept my schoolwork on task consistently.

And I loved my classes. Not only did I love them, but I was also really good at them. I could see myself as a lawyer, defending the poor and downtrodden. After all, the poor and downtrodden weren't just imagination to me. Talk about them, and you were talking about my birth mother. Who wouldn't want a chance to help other women like my birth mother have a fair shot in a system that was stacked against them?

I marked an important milestone my senior year. I had my own little room, which I was excited about because it really was the only time until that point that I'd had a room of my own. Those of you who had your own room growing up don't know the way that having your own space just relaxes you. You can let your guard down completely when you're alone in a way you can't around even the nicest family member or friend.

That year, I experienced that kind of freedom and peace for the first time. I felt so grown up, being responsible for my own space. I didn't have to answer to anyone when I closed that door.

Don't get me wrong—I am and always have been an extro-vert. I flourish on connection. No one was more surprised than I was to find that I also found benefit in solitude.

College stayed pretty much within a rhythm of work, school, teaching fitness, planning and attending parties, and going home to work for the next year until I turned twenty-one. Until then, it was understood that if you drank at a party, you were just going with the flow.

That changed for me when I turned twenty-one. After my driver's license declared me legal, I belonged to the group of people who could order a mimosa or two with brunch, margaritas with nachos, and wine with dinner. I could also stop by the liquor store and plunk down my credit card for a couple of bottles of Tito's if I was having a hard time with finals.

This change started a pattern of negotiation for me. Do your work, and you can drink. I followed that pattern for most of my early adulthood.

I didn't do this all the time. But when I indulged, I went hard. This wasn't abnormal behavior in college, where a lot of the social life is built around drinking. But it was a dangerous habit for me to cultivate. And it shone a light on another dangerous habit, too.

The purity culture that had been preached to me from childhood on had clashed spectacularly with my hormones and desire for connection in high school. Add to that the constant trumpeting of my birth mother as a bad girl and the traumatic loss of my virginity through rape, and I had a complicated sexual history.

I couldn't escape the fact that my first sexual experience had happened while I was drunk and passed out. I didn't want to miss the connection of being physical with someone I liked. But past experience, hidden by my brain to protect me, led me to get blind drunk before taking someone to bed. My body remembered and recreated that experience, even if I didn't, because I hadn't healed from it.

I wonder how different this time in my life might have been if I had been able to report the rape that happened when I was fourteen. If I had told my parents and gotten therapy then, how might I have approached sex in a healthier way when I was old enough to choose it for myself? If I had seen the man who violated me punished for what he did, what might that act of justice have done for my self-esteem?

Those are questions I can't answer. That's a reality that didn't happen for me. All I can do is look at the fourteen-year-old child I was, so steeped in expectations of abandonment and punishment by her early life, and send her love.

When we don't heal, no amount of coping will erase our trauma. All the coping does is to numb us or distract us for a while. But all the while, the trauma is there, waiting, sending our souls and bodies messages like unhappiness and physical pain.

The sooner we put aside our coping tools and look directly at our trauma, the sooner we can begin healing. Naming and dealing with what hurt us is hard; I'm not going to lie. But there is no other alternative. There is only wasting time.

Heartbreak

A bright spot in my college career was being able to live at the International House, a row house on Vernon Street with a beautiful porch where I liked to sit in the big white rocking chairs. Because my birth mother had been an immigrant, I qualified, although I had lived most of my life in white suburbs. I was really proud that I got myself into that house. There, I felt like I was celebrating my Cuban heritage.

This environment was exactly the right one for me. I thrived around people from different backgrounds who spoke different languages and thought differently about life in America and around the globe. They opened my eyes to the world in a whole new way.

When college was drawing to an end, I was in an enviable position. George Mason School of Law was offering me a partial scholarship. I was graduating at the top of my class as class president. I would even give a speech to my schoolmates about the opportunities ahead of us.

But something felt wrong to me. I recognized this sense of loneliness despite my achievements because it was how I had felt when I was graduating high school. I needed a mother to say, "I'm proud of you. You did a great job. You're a spectacular person."

No matter how I longed to hear them, I knew better than to expect those words from Mom. She didn't feel them, and she wouldn't say what she didn't feel. She was honest like that. So that left me one other option. I had to speak to Barbara Valdez.

I always knew I could contact my birth mother through my social worker, which was what I did. I called social services to have a call set up. And one day at the end of my college career, my cell phone rang. When I picked it up, I heard this woman speaking broken English. Though I didn't speak Spanish, I immediately knew who she was: Barbara Valdez. My heart went out to her. Through her tears, she told me, "I am so sorry. Life was hard for me, and it never got easier. I tried, and I kept on messing up. I was failing so much, and I failed you." She told me that she felt like she was drowning. And then she told me what I now know of her story.

Barbara Valdez got to America between April and October of 1980 from her home in Havana, Cuba. She was swept up into a mass exodus of ten thousand Cubans who stormed the Peruvian Embassy on April 4–5 seeking asylum. They were rebelling against Fidel Castro's dictatorship.

Hearing and understanding their pleas, the Peruvian Embassy allowed the protestors to remain within their walls, refusing to turn over the "unpatriotic Cubans" to ruthless political enforcers. The protest dragged on for weeks, with thousands of people camping without any supplies on the ten-acre embassy campus. They relieved themselves on the ground and stripped the mango trees, including the leaves, to relieve their hunger.

As a result of Castro's embarrassment in front of world leaders, he agreed to let the rebels leave. Eventually, 120,000 Cubans departed from Cuba's crowded Mariel Harbor during that summer and fall. Those waiting to leave were strip searched for smuggled goods.

These refugees were then left in a filthy tent camp called El Mosquito, where the usual horrors of refugees waited for them. Food arrived haphazardly, and no one had made provision for sanitation. Disease spread through the camp. Guards preyed on the protestors, beating some and raping others at random.

A trickle of refugees began leaving on April 19, as generous Cuban Americans sailed from Florida to rescue relatives and anyone else they could cram aboard. Barbara bravely set a new course for herself in a new land as one of 60 to 80 unbathed people who were smashed together like sardines on little fishing boats that comfortably held maybe 30–50 people.

How she survived once she arrived, I do not know. She did not have family to show her how to get around or how to navigate the language. During the racy 1980s, rampant cocaine and prostitution were ravaging Miami, making it a hot spot for human trafficking and other crime.

My birth mother met Oscar and got caught up with him in a dangerous life that revolved around drugs. She brought me into the world in July 1983 at Jackson Hospital in Miami Dade County. My brother was born 11 months after me. And because of the life she was living with Oscar, she was separated from both of us before we knew her.

Because it had been so long since my birth mother had seen me, she wanted to tell me everything. After she finished telling me about her history, she told me that she was gay. Immediately, I felt walls go up. I was Catholic. How could I accept a gay mother? I couldn't.

I dissociated. I wasn't ready to have that conversation. I told her: "It's okay," because I wanted it to be okay. But it felt like too much.

After my birth mother finished telling me her life story, I told her, "I'm graduating from college, and I am class president." She said, "I'm so proud of you. I've always said you're a leader. You've always been my lion."

Those words warmed my heart. They were what I needed to hear. She gave me what I needed when I needed it most.

But that one phone call did not lead to a relationship. Too much time had passed, and we didn't even speak the same language. Sadly, we had missed the chance during my childhood to know each other deeply, and this talk felt like closure more than anything else.

Some parts of our past don't need to come with us into the future. All we need to do is make peace with them. For me, this phone call was the peace I needed. Barbara Valdez had sparked in me some understanding and compassion—compassion that would grow as I reconsidered what my birth mother and I had both said. With that, I could go forward into my adult life.

NEEDS

When I graduated college and was truly out on my own, I created a life around me that fulfilled my needs. I learned over the years what I truly needed and how to meet those needs in healthier ways. But the story of this part of my life is me meeting those needs in unhealthy ways. Eventually, something would happen to me to stop a destructive pattern.

What about you? If you see some unhealthy patterns in your own life, it helps to look behind the behavior to the need. What needs do you have that you might be meeting in destructive ways?

Success

George Mason School of Law was a welcome challenge. My college had prepared me well to handle the logic and memorization that I would need in studying the law. I could have tackled all the courses ahead of me, I have no doubt.

What I chose not to tackle was the astronomical debt that mounted daily. Though I went to only one semester, I ended up a hundred thousand dollars in the hole. After some soul searching, I decided that I just didn't want to be a lawyer that badly. My inner foster child had needed me to become rich and successful. Fine. I could do that without bankrupting myself in the process.

At this crossroads in my life, a headhunter approached me with an offer. Corporate Executive Board was a best practice research firm that served Fortune 500 companies, and which eventually merged with Gardner. I was a good fit for their sales team.

I sold to CFOs and general counsel. I was million-dollar marketer three years in a row. I was good at my job.

This opportunity promised to provide me two things I wanted: a challenge and a commission. I took all my positive energy and relentless determination and went to work. Within a year, I paid off my hundred-thousand-dollar student debt.

Nevertheless, I entered an environment where drinking was the culture. While working there, the more success I achieved, the more incentive checks I received, which meant Happy Hours, restaurants, and traveling. Everything picked up speed and magnitude, not just drinking.

But I didn't handle the social drinking well. The company sent me on several trips as rewards for hitting sales goals. Through indulging too much, I left myself open for attack by a bunch of white female colleagues who did not like me and who were intimidated by someone they saw as competition. Seeing me drink like that gave them something to use against me. As an attractive woman of color who became louder than life when I had too much to drink, I put a target on my back.

One of the first incidents that these shady ladies were able to report was the first trip I won as a top sales executive, a trip to the Dominican Republic. Here I was in my twenties, at the top of my game, living my life, and having a ball. Together with the other ladies from CEB, all white, I had been drinking Long Island Iced Teas and rum mixed with Coke at the swim-up pool bar all day.

One redhead, Susie, saw that I was drunk, just like everyone else, and decided that I was too trashed to enjoy a sunset cruise, one of the excursions provided to the employees.

"You, know, you really should just stay back at the hotel and sleep," she suggested, dripping with synthetic sweetness. "Go ahead. Take the night off."

"Okay, thanks," I told her. I didn't know that she'd asked me alone, not the other white women who were equally trashed, to stay off the ship.

Once we got back home, Susie made sure that my drinking, not hers or anyone else's, got back to my boss, R.P. She made it sound like I was the only one who had been drunk that night. No—I was just the only one she asked not to go on the cruise.

So, R.P. pulled me into his office and told me the importance of drinking in a way that wouldn't look bad for myself or the company. I took his advice and cooled out on socializing with my co-workers, especially since it had become clear they were watching me. And I couldn't trust them.

One thing I didn't recognize at the time was that I might have been drinking partly to check out of those work gatherings. I was devoting a massive amount of time and energy to doing a job that wasn't my calling. Sure, I enjoyed some aspects of it, but it didn't draw on my talents and desires fully. And no amount of money can make up for long for doing what you are not meant to do. Especially doing that kind of work around people you can't trust who don't really like you.

The binge drinking incidents that started around that time did not meet my definition of alcoholism or substance abuse. I didn't see them that way, not even after I crashed a car while driving drunk. Per usual, I was with some colleagues celebrating during happy hour, and I had one too many. I needed to get home because I was scheduled to leave town the next morning. Unfortunately, sometimes you don't know how drunk you are until it is too late.

I was leaving D.C. driving on the E Street ramp to 66 West, toward Virginia. I didn't realize that the car in front of me had stopped until I ran into him. I knew enough to know that if the police got there and tested my blood alcohol level, I would be in trouble; so, I left. I grabbed as much of my work stuff as I could and got out of there. I must have grabbed my keys, too, because I had them to get into my apartment.

Once I was home, I totally blacked out. The next morning when it was time to leave, I didn't realize that I had left my purse with my driver's license behind in the wrecked car until I couldn't find my driver's license. Luckily, I got onto the plane with my passport.

When I returned from my trip, my answering machine was flooded with calls from the police, who had my pocketbook. Again, I just got off with a warning, probably because my last name, Sobczak, did not identify me as a woman of color. I'm sure that staying at the site of the accident to be seen and tested would have netted me a different outcome.

I didn't think I had a problem with alcohol because I wasn't drinking secretly. I was a successful woman who turned to drink as my reward. Looking back, I'm amazed that I handled everything that I did, like teaching fitness classes on my lunch hour. I would leave work, change fast, work out with my students, change back, and hit work again without missing a step.

This accident, however, made me miss a step. This outside force interrupted my belief that everything was under control. And it made me slow my drinking for a while.

Strength

While I was working in corporate America, I found body-building as a discipline. I needed a challenge; I was outperforming the competition where I was. Working with Fortune 500 companies didn't feel hard for me. It didn't require all of who I was.

I threw myself into a physical challenge. I was far from out of shape; in fact, I was pretty fit. But bodybuilding took me to another level. I hired a trainer, and within a few months, I lost thirty pounds. I placed second in my first show.

The way I could sculpt and shape my muscles in specific ways amazed me. I felt powerful and fierce when I trained so hard, knowing that I was accomplishing something few people could or would do. I determined to take this discipline as far as I could go. I would devote myself to it.

Dad would come to these events to cheer me on. It meant a lot to me that he would take the time to be there for me. Just like when I was a little girl on the soccer field, I looked for his face and listened for his voice, and knowing he was there warmed my heart.

Competitions took a lot of work. After exercising with a trainer to get to peak competition readiness physically, I would prepare the icing on the cake, the beauty elements. Then I would go to the venue on the day and bring it all together.

I liked dressing up for competitions, too. It was a chance to go all out on my hair, nails, and makeup, and to select a range of outfits. These competitions weren't beauty pageants. If you didn't display the required physique, no amount of mascara on earth was going to save you. But if things were pretty close, some beauty could sway a decision.

Depending on the level, these competitions happened in school gyms, community centers, and other auditoriums, anywhere with a stage, good lights, and a sound system. The smaller venues hosted smaller, local competitions. They might cover a few cities or a few counties, depending on the number of competitors to apply, and the event itself might take a few hours. Then you would advance to regional competitions, which covered a grouping of states. Winners of those competitions went on to nationals, which would often take place at resorts or convention centers over the span of four or five days. Once the audience lights went down and the competition began, the venue didn't really matter. Everyone's eyes were on stage. The lights flashed red in patterns against a background to increase the sensuality of the competitors' appearances. Hype, upbeat music set the expectation that the women coming on stage were about to blow everyone's minds.

There were several divisions of bodybuilding, each one showcasing a particular body type. Your genes, which determined the way your body layered muscle on your frame, would often determine the category where you could do well. The Wellness category, which expected thicker leg muscles, worked well with my Cuban physique. With Wellness, you were going for an asymmetrical look—smaller up top and bigger on the bottom. On the other hand, the Figure category expected you to be wide up top and straight down on the bottom. That was not me and never was going to be. But I could rock Wellness!

One by one, the contestants would come forward and pose to upbeat music in specific ways, highlighting the tone and definition of a particular muscle group. When one person's turn was done, she'd head backstage so that the next contestant could show the same pose. Then all the contestants would return and hit the same pose so that the judges could compare the definition of specific muscle groupings from contestant to contestant. Then everyone headed backstage to change into another outfit. We'd repeat this for perhaps five different poses. Then other groups in other categories would do the same thing.

Let me tell you—I invested in some spectacularly sparkly bikinis! And we're not even going to mention the eyelashes, hair extensions, and acrylic nails. Ordinarily, I didn't need any fake tan because of my Cuban genes. But in the bodybuilding world, all the contestants have to get professionally painted, even those with the darkest skin tones, because under the stage lights the judges can't see the musculature without the artificial tan.

I won some, and I lost some. Competing taught me a lot about myself. One thing I learned was that I didn't like the actual competing as much as I liked the preparation. In fact, I got such a huge case of the nerves during one contest in April 2020 that after my turn was over, I ran off stage and out the door. I felt sick and scared, and I didn't like feeling that way. It took a while for me to calm down enough to return for the prize announcements.

In the gym, I never felt those kinds of nerves. There, I had a fantastic time, every time I showed up. It became clear to me that I was really in the competition cycle to challenge myself and see what I could accomplish physically. That was some good information for me.

It was also good information for me to note that this competition was my first sober show. During my earlier competition prep when I was in my twenties, I was not attending AA meetings or even thinking I was an alcoholic. I was using competitions to control my drinking.

When I jumped back into competing during the pandemic in 2020, I was attending AA meetings and prepping for a show at the same time, which was a totally different experience. I was much healthier, sound in mind and body.

For the first time, no substances were running through my system to dull my responses or my emotions. I could really feel what I was feeling in a way I never had before. No wonder things felt overwhelming! They were all new to me. Now I get to do both training and competition regularly in an empowering way.

When we find something that lights us up and brings out the best in us, it's important to experience it fully. Coping mechanisms, so useful in shielding us from the pain of trauma, can also rob us of true joy. That's why healing is so important. It literally gives us back the best of our lives.

Independence

Around the time the housing crisis hit America, my time in corporate sales came to a close. Corporate Executive Board was laying off employees, and my number came up. I was so scared. I wondered what I was supposed to do with myself now. Did I want to seek another corporate position? If I was honest, I knew that I didn't.

Fitness motivated me and made me happy. The answer had been plain to me, though I hadn't had the mindset to see it.

What had I given up sleepovers and trips to the mall to do as a young teen? Teach step classes. What had I given up my lunch breaks to do while I worked my corporate job? Teach classes at gym. Clearly, helping other people reach their physical goals was close to my heart.

But how was I supposed to make ends meet as a trainer? Could I make enough? Was this really the right move for me?

To cover my bills and to test this new direction, I started working every spare moment. Between Gold's Gym and Washington Sports Club, I worked eighty hours a week. No hungry law-school intern ever took work more seriously.

I consulted several people, who all confirmed what I knew. And while I visited Dad and Aunt Leslie, I talked to them. They saw how happy I was working in fitness. They loved me and believed in me, and they knew me well enough to give me the right advice.

True to form, Dad coached me on the practicalities of running my own business. But he agreed that I had hit on something that fit me. And Aunt Leslie came up with the perfect name for my new business.

"You should call it FitNez. You know, fitness plus your name." Her eyes sparkled with the idea, and as soon as I heard it, I knew it was right.

Running my own business was a hustle from the start. I did what I needed to do, whether that was strictly allowed or not. There are certain gyms which only want designated staff training members, but I couldn't always abide by those restrictions. I needed space and clients. I was going to get them. Inez did not fail.

I did every job. I scheduled. I kept the books. I even built my own website!

And man, did I learn to watch every penny! I was determined to do things the right way as far as paying taxes and getting a business license. Sometimes that felt like a penalty instead of participation in the American way, but I did it. I was scrappy!

And I felt such a sense of freedom in beginning this business. It wasn't just that I was working for myself. I was free from the expectations of my inner foster child that I could only be successful if I went into medicine or law. I was free to be successful doing what I loved.

My clients started becoming a larger and larger part of my life. When you train someone, things get personal pretty quickly. From the beginning, when I was doing physical training primarily, I still discussed nutrition and lifestyle habits. You can't discuss topics like those without getting into deep thoughts, desires, and experiences.

People need comfort and wholeness. When you're a trainer, you see the results of people taking shortcuts to happiness. When I see someone who's out of shape, I see a whole history that needs to be addressed.

This side of my work appealed to me from the start. But the money didn't follow that part of the business at first. People wanted to pay for workout coaching, and I was qualified to offer that service. So that's where a lot of my effort centered at first.

I talked about my desires to be there for people and talk about feelings and behaviors and eating decisions with one client, Victoria, who came to be a good friend. A former tri-athlete, Victoria was really successful in her own sales and marketing business. I trusted her advice.

"You've got to follow the money, Inez," she told me. "Diversify your income streams, but give people what they want."

"I don't like to think I'm giving up on the part of my job I like the best," I said.

"Hey, don't worry about that right now! Little by little, you'll build up that part of what you do. But you have to stay strong to get there. Do the workouts. The coaching will come."

Victoria was right. The short discussions I had with my clients about why they might not see the progress they wanted evolved into formal coaching sessions soon enough. Life is holistic. You can't ever perfect just one part without paying attention to the rest. You have to balance your efforts.

Soon I had enough stability in my business to find a formal location. I rented a little studio above a Papa John's pizza place. Trust me, the irony is not lost on me that I was so close to serious calorie temptation for my clients. In fact, I used that location to set them at ease.

I'd tell them, "If you ever think about quitting, you can always just go downstairs."

They knew what I was telling them. I understood that calorie-dense food choices were everywhere. I also believed in their power to choose their health—to walk upstairs to do the hard work instead of staying on the ground floor to chow down.

With a lot of time, faith, sweat, and patience, I built FitNez into something really solid. Satisfied clients introduced me to people who needed me, so that I soon had a waiting list.

However, until the coaching portion of my business grew bigger, I did find ways to help people with other habits at the same time. Ironically, although I was deep into a cycle of abusing alcohol when my own personal pain overwhelmed me, I added helping others with sobriety as part of what I offered.

I had no idea how personal this part of my work would soon become.

Love

One coaching client came to me after having been in an accident. He was in recovery from alcohol abuse, and while healing, he had gained weight. It was easy to substitute comfort food and inactivity for the oblivion of alcohol, and now he needed help to beat these habits.

That client was Brian, and I enjoyed his company from the start. He had a great sense of humor, and he was a good listener, too. Most of all, he respected me and listened to me. He really took me seriously and trusted me to do my job well.

With my help, Brian lost the weight he wanted to lose and gained some great new habits. I was really proud of him for sticking to his nutrition and exercise plan the way he had stuck with his sobriety. It took a lot of discipline to achieve what he did.

We started hanging out as friends, going to dinner or the movies or out to the club to dance. Feelings started to develop on his end, feelings I didn't know at first if I could reciprocate. He was attractive; it was just that I didn't date many white guys. And Brian wasn't just white. He was upper crust, part of the Arlington country-club set. Having come from a white family myself, I knew that these people were out of my class and out of my family's class.

But one day, he picked me up from the airport, and things just clicked between us. For the first time, I felt what he felt. We went back to his place and had dinner, and I just didn't leave. We were a couple from then on.

My parents were thrilled. In accepting Brian, I had finally done something that they wholeheartedly approved. He was exactly the kind of person they wanted for me. I was surprised by their enthusiasm.

Brian and I spent a lot of time together, and I could see where things were heading. We were at that age where life pushes you in a certain direction. The direction life was pushing us was towards marriage and family.

And I wanted to settle down. A child of such turmoil and uncertainty early in my life, I found a lot of appeal in the idea of creating my own family. At the same time, something inside me doubted that I could be happy within his world. Could I really be an Arlington housewife, concerned with lawn maintenance, charity functions, and social events? Could I find purpose in a world where I would never be white enough to pass, where I and my children would always look just a little different?

While I was still pondering these questions, Brian popped the question, the big one. And what was I supposed to say? I loved him. I liked him. I could see a future with him. Were my doubts enough reason to hurt him and reject him? They weren't.

I told him yes. Then I started planning my wedding.

I look back at the newly engaged woman that I was then, and I wish I could hold her hand and talk to her. She was so lost and still trying so desperately to be good, to make her parents proud, and to succeed. I wish I could tell her that she was trying too hard in the wrong places. The real work she needed to do was not choosing flower arrangements and booking a hotel event venue. The real work was sitting down with her own heart and looking hard at her own pain, her own desires, and her own deepest needs.

Besides the crisis of my own personal issues, I had a hard time with all the pre-wedding social expectations. There were all these engagement celebrations with dinners and drinks. I was drinking consistently from Thursday to Sunday on a weekly basis. This is when I started again to black out all the time and make bad choices. During this time, I did not like myself. I didn't like that I was lying all the time. I was fighting with my friends. I was drinking excessively, and I was having health issues.

But still, I went to Kleinfeld 's in New York, which was pretty awesome. If you have watched *Say Yes to the Dress*, you can imagine the wonderful time I had being shown lovely dress after lovely dress. The party I brought with me had a VIP concierge service while we looked at all the different creations.

I remember trying them all on and loving them. I thought I wanted a fitted, sexy mermaid dress, but then I put on this one dress: white with lace, little crystals, and pearls glittering all over it. It was strapless with a beautiful, cinched belt that tied at the waist, and when I put it on, I felt like the skirt of my dress was a wedding bell. A delicate, floating veil misted my hair. I looked like the little girl I had been at her first communion, all grown up.

While I stood at the mirror in this dress, the woman who was assisting me whispered into my ear: "What could you see your father walking you down the aisle in?" Her question to me solidified my choice.

I picked my wedding dress because I thought of what Dad wanted to see me get married in. I wanted his approval, and I got it. A picture of me in my dress is his phone home screen.

But I was confused. I started an affair during my engagement that I thought might be my future. Before the marriage, I told my best friend Jamie that I needed to call the wedding off. She thought that I needed to go through with the wedding. How did I know that marriage wasn't what I wanted if I was just going to run away from it? Everyone thought my intuition was just wedding jitters.

My drive to be responsible and not to let other people down finally decided me. I pushed all my fears to one side and said, "I do." That day, I felt like I was walking through a dream.

One morning a few months into my marriage, I was lying in bed with Brian after a night of drinking. He turned over, looked me right in my face, and confronted me about my affair. Surprised and guilty, I got up quickly out of bed and got dressed.

I left, went across the street to a restaurant, and lied to the waitress, telling her that someone in my family had passed, because I didn't want to say that I was about to get a divorce. It was the first time I consciously told a lie to drink the way I wanted to drink because I didn't want to feel.

At that time, I was using drink and relationships to hide the emotions that would have guided me in the right way. I was looking at what people expected or wanted out of me instead of listening to myself. And ignoring myself meant that I ended up hurting myself and others.

Connection

After my six-month marriage ended, one way I healed was by going back to my roots. I took a spontaneous trip to my mother's birthplace: Havana, Cuba. I had been staying in Arlington, sleeping on a friend's couch. One morning I just woke up and asked her, "Come with me to Cuba." I felt the need to fly out of the country, away from my shame, sadness, and anger.

At that time, it was really uncommon to travel to Cuba. We had to have an educational or cultural reason to go. I found an Art and Culture trip to Cuba, which served as a passport into the country for me and my friend. Excited, we flew to Miami.

From Miami, we hopped on a 20-minute flight and landed in a new, seemingly untouched country where it seemed that time had stood still. Caribbean heat settled on our skin as we walked across graveled pavers down a row of antique cars from the 1940s and 50s waiting to take guests on a tour of old town Havana.

I kept hearing the word "fuerte," the Spanish word for strong, from Cuban people looking at me. Everyone we met also kept on saying "rostro Cubano" which means "Cuban face." I had never identified as truly Cuban except with my license plate and on paper in college, when being Cuban allowed me entry into the International House. Here, in the place of my mother's origin, I was no longer "other;" I was the woman with the Cuban face.

I felt an immense pride. I thought to myself, "I really am Cuban. And the Cubans think I'm Cuban. I must belong here, to them."

That sense of being recognized and included was what I had been looking for my whole life. I had always longed for someone to say, "You look like you belong here with us." I never had anyone say that in any room I'd ever been in. But in Cuba, the people saw me in a way I had not even seen myself. I spent five days soaking up my culture, my identity, and my roots. Here was an entire island of my extended family.

Thinking back on it, that acknowledgment of myself as a Cuban probably was the only way my ancestors knew I was ready to meet them, which is the second thing that happened. At this crossroads of my life, when I had lost a future that was not mine and when I had found a people that wanted me, I met my spiritual guide.

Here's what happened. To challenge myself, I joined a group of tourists and ran the Malecón, a concrete wall in Old Havana built to prevent erosion. To keep the sea from washing away the six-lane avenue and sidewalk where Cubans meet and greet one another, the Malecon stretches eight kilometers from the mouth of Havana Harbor to the mouth of the Almendares River.

The night before the run, I was super drunk. Partly because I desperately wanted to fit in with people who looked like me, I had drunk all this rum and smoked all these Cuban cigars. It made for the worst hangover in the morning. It was so painful. I should have stopped drinking right then!

Stumbling about, hung over, with one eye open, I found people talking about this challenging run. One guy told me: "If you're going to run the Malecón, you need to do it before 6:00 AM because it gets hot."

"No problem," I thought. "I can do that. I've got a few hours before sunrise." I told the others I would see them at breakfast.

While the sun was still barely peeking over the horizon, I dragged myself out of my hangover. Having never gone to bed that night, I downed cups of coffee to counteract the exhaustion and the alcohol. The only reason I even did the run is that I really take a lot of pride in doing what I say I am going to do. That was it.

While I did avoid the full intensity of the sun's rays by starting early, the sun still beat me as I ran panting with alcohol draining through my sweat. I couldn't believe how a place could roast you at this time in the morning. On the way back, the sun's heat really affected me. I was sweating and tasting the heat. If I closed and opened my mouth, I was sure flames would have escaped. I could see the sun tracing tan marks on my arms and legs as I watched. I was so happy to reach the end!

While walking along a cobbled path back to my hotel, I scooted around a shaded corner, searching for any relief. I saw a small chapel and felt compelled to go through the doors. Once I was inside, I saw a place on the right where I could kneel and put in a dollar with my prayer.

I knew I needed to pray. I should absolve my sins, atone for my actions that had caused the end of my marriage. I found a pew and sat there. Then I fought a losing battle to quiet my sobs as I kneeled before Jesus and prayed that he would forgive me, because I couldn't forgive myself.

As my head bent in penance, out of nowhere I felt a woman behind me place her gentle hands on my shoulders. The comfort of her hands let me weep without judgment. This woman, who felt instantly familiar to me, was hugging me near, making me feel safe.

After her fingers loosened their grip, I figured I needed to pull it together because I at least needed to introduce myself and say thank you. When I got myself together to turn around to thank her, she was not there. I looked around, confused.

I asked the janitor, who came in at 7:00 AM: "Where did the old lady go?"

He answered in his broken English, "I'm the only one in here. No one's come in. No one's come out."

The hairs on my neck stood up a little when I asked him again: "You sure? There was a woman sitting behind me."

His blank stare helped the reality of the moment settle in. I got it.

And after that moment, I knew that I was not alone. I was going to be fine, despite the pain. Knowing that my guide saw me and showed up for me, I was able to march through that hard moment in my life because of her saving hands on my shoulders.

Support

Real connection with friends I can trust is one of my number one needs. I'm a people person, and genuine sharing and empathy are like air to me. When I felt uncertain about being myself or when I was just feeling stress and wanted to relax, I relied on alcohol to make that connection for me. I didn't want the alcohol for itself; I wanted what it was going to give me.

Back home in D.C., I gradually began to spend time with people I met outside work. One friend, Orlando, taught Latin dance classes at several clubs, and I loved learning from him. That kind of movement and music felt like a tangible connection to my heritage, like I was making up for some of the cultural erasure I had suffered. I met great people at his classes.

The gym was another great way to meet people. The people I met at gym I knew shared some of my values about health and activity, but other than that baseline, they were from a great variety of backgrounds and cultures. Many of them became friends for a while; some still are friends.

I met some people when I was out partying. Dancing was one of my favorite things to do, and I regularly invited people out to dance with me at one club or another. If the music was good and the people were friendly, I could think of few better ways to spend an evening.

Right before my twenty-fifth birthday, I met one of my closest friends at one of these clubs. I had been there for only a little while when I noticed how good the music was. I had to see who was working this magic, and so I found the DJ and introduced myself.

That DJ was Azam, and I quickly hired him to do the music for my upcoming twenty-fifth birthday. The party was on fire, partly because of his handiwork. From then on, I made sure to find out where he was working when I wanted to go out. Then we started meeting outside the club sometimes for dinner or drinks.

I found that Azam was not only a talented DJ and a lot of fun to hang out with, but he was also a sincerely kind and genuine person. Though the question of romance arose early in our relationship, we soon agreed that we were like family. He felt like my brother, and I trusted him absolutely. I'm still lucky that I walked into that club where he was playing that first night.

But I did not honor our friendship well when Azam was getting married. His wife Joy, a professional stylist and talent agent, booked an elegant vineyard for her bachelorette party and hired a limousine to provide transportation there. Though she and I were not close at that time, she invited me as a favor to Azam. It was an extremely kind gesture on her part.

Perhaps the upcoming wedding of someone that I cared about brought up my own failed marriage in a way that hit me emotionally. Maybe a lot of things were converging that made this party just the final thing that I couldn't handle right then. All I know is that I was leaning hard on my coping mechanism.

I showed up to Joy's apartment already pretty much the worse for wear. I grabbed a bottle off the table she had available for refreshments, and I took it with me to the venue, sipping all the way. By the time we arrived, I was sobbing and loud, and I made a humiliating scene. It ended with my passing out in the limousine and missing the rest of the bachelorette party, which I had effectively ruined.

This event was not isolated. My inner pain was causing me to spiral: to drink, black out, and act in other ways that endangered me. I was trying to keep things together, but life was hard.

Stung and embarrassed by my messy divorce, my family radiated disapproval whenever I saw them. Jamie was a constant in my life, but she was far away in Lynchburg. Debra was concentrating on her own family and her wellness. We had never quite come back together from the distance that had crept into our relationship.

Slowly, it became apparent to me that all my friends were people I held at arm's length. Each one knew a piece of me. Some, like Jamie, knew a whole lot of the real me from way back. But I let no one all the way in. I did not confide all my messy emotions and all my joys and all my inner thoughts to my friends.

They showed up for me when I needed them to connect, to dance, to party, to have a good time. But my early life had taught me that no one was forever, that no one stayed, and that no one truly loved me for myself, only for what I could do or give. My trauma, eating away at me like a spiritual cancer, was for me alone to bear.

This is one reason why I did not react well when I heard that my college friend Emefa was planning to put together a group of close friends for an intervention. I knew that each person was going to take turns looking me in the eye and saying, "We think your drinking has gotten bad." But these people didn't know all of me. They would be judging me without true understanding.

At that time, because I was in such a state of shame about how I coped, I took offense to the idea of sitting through accusations. All my old patterns and stories of "they're going to leave me" or "I'm not good enough" surfaced. As a result, I went individually to the people Emefa had approached and told each one that I was fine. I didn't want that intervention to happen.

I think I might have reacted differently if the intervention had occurred one on one. If one of those people, say Emefa because she was so worried, had sat me down, expressed real concern and care, and asked how she could help, I might have listened.

Have you ever done something like this? Have you pushed away people who were concerned for you because you were embarrassed or hurt? It's a hard place to be. After all, if you were healthy enough to handle the criticism well, you probably wouldn't be doing things to worry the people close to you.

But we need those people. As hard as it is to hear their concern, we need to listen. Chances are, they're saying something your inner self already knows. They're giving it a voice.

At that time, I couldn't listen. Instead, because of my childhood trauma and insecurities, I created distance from the people that I needed to speak into my life. I took offense to people who were offering advice, encouragement, and friendship just when I most needed those things. Missing genuine support, I fell into real danger.

Safety

I learned the hard way that drinking was endangering my safety. One evening, I'd been at a party, and while there, I continued the drinking I'd been doing earlier that day. I honestly don't remember much of the party because I was on autopilot.

When it was time to go, I called a rideshare. (Hey, at least I wasn't driving). But the driver who showed up would have had to be blind not to see that I was in bad shape, unsteady and shaky. He took me home and got me inside. I don't remember much about that part. I think I remember shutting the door in his face.

What I do remember was waking up that night knowing that something was wrong. Immediately, I saw that my MacBook and a blanket were missing. Someone was in my apartment, and that someone was a stranger. I rolled out of bed and got to my feet with the silence of sheer panic.

Somehow, I had the phone in my hand, and I called the police. Soon, I heard sirens outside my building. Instead of passing like they did regularly all night in D.C., they paused, and I saw blue and red lights swirling across the ceiling, shining through the window.

The man in my apartment fled, pulling the door closed as he left. Soon the police arrived. They took notes and examined the place. They couldn't find any signs of forced entry. No, I told them. I wasn't sure I had locked the door earlier.

At this point, they began to talk among themselves, and I understood that I had moved off the high priority list. They were having doubts that there had ever been an emergency. If one had existed legitimately before, it was certainly not there now.

Later, after the police left and I went back to sleep with a firmly locked door to guard me, I felt the encounter as dream-like and unbelievable. How could I be sure anything had happened besides the fact that my property was missing?

I went to the building management and asked for the security tapes of that night. Boom! There he was, the rideshare driver who had dropped me off earlier that night. He was leaving right after I had heard someone moving around in my apartment, and he was carrying my MacBook and blanket. It had happened. There was proof.

How could this driver still be employed? Surely, I wasn't the first vulnerable passenger he'd returned to attack. But would I be believed by the rideshare company? I hadn't been in the best state when I'd entered the car, and the driver would bring that fact to his defense if I raised the issue.

I let a few days pass. Then I told a handful of friends what had happened. They expressed sympathy, but I saw something in their eyes. Doubt. Suspicion. That was what I saw, with the people I loved and trusted the most. And the guardedness in their eyes convinced me that I was not going to pursue this man. After all, if the people who loved me didn't believe me, how would anyone else?

Blackouts like those put me in dangerous or uncomfortable situations. I had cultivated a group of friends: people I knew I could trust to get me home safe when I couldn't trust myself. But one of my watchers was taking advantage, and I wasn't able to connect the dots until it was much too late.

For a long time, I had thought Ted was truly on my side. He had watched over me, stayed in touch, and kept me in his life. He was one of the people I trusted to get me home safe.

It was only after my sobriety that I was able to piece together an incident that happened months prior because I was blacked out when it happened. We had been hanging out drinking, and I passed out in his bed. This was not unusual. I had done this several times before, and he never touched me.

This time, I woke up to see him in his white sleeveless undershirt positioning himself to get on top of me. I was able to push him away and pretend like I didn't know what he was trying to do. Once I became sober, I asked him about what had happened. I thought he would be honest about it. He wasn't.

I realized this incident was something different and that the events didn't add up to what he recalled. What I recalled was drinking too much at his Super Bowl party and saying, "Hey, I'm going to bed."

But talking to him afterward, I said, "I remember my clothes being on when I went to bed. Why were my clothes off?"

He said, "No. Your clothes were on."

But I couldn't let this go. He couldn't just gaslight me. I had to know who was safe and who wasn't. So, I insisted right back.

"You did, because I wouldn't have gone to your bed and taken off all my clothes." People were still at his house; I would not have taken off my clothes in front of these other people. I knew this for sure.

We never got to any resolution, any admission. But I took him off my mental list of safe people. In return, he started telling people that I was a habitual liar.

You know what? During the time he knew me, I was. He knew me at one of the unhealthiest times of my life, when I had not done the deep soul work to heal and live in honesty.

I have now. And I know what I know. And the fact that we are not communicating now that I am a healthy person speaks volumes about why he hung around me and what exactly was in our friendship for him.

For our own health and safety, we need to acknowledge the dangers that come from our coping mechanisms. It's so easy to brush them off, to say that we can handle them or that they're not that serious. But naming those risks and telling ourselves the truth about them is an important part of healing.

Motherhood

In one part of my life, I was successful, healthy, and focused on others and their welfare. I was a successful entrepreneur.

Also, I had a circle of friends who cared about me as much as I let them.

In the other part of my life, I was running towards oblivion. Along with drinking, men were a reliable source of oblivion for me. I dated around, never staying with anyone for long. After the disaster of my divorce, I didn't want to commit to anyone for a long time. One of the men I started dating at that time was Chad.

This was not a great time for me to meet anyone serious. Chad and I weren't approaching life or each other with the ability to build a good foundation. Had our son Xavier not arrived to cement that bond permanently, Chad would have been another story about a crazy time in my life. But some choices are forever, and you don't know that when you're making them.

Soon after the intervention planned by my friends, I got pregnant. In a way, it was great news, and perfect timing. I could stop drinking for the length of this pregnancy and say, "Look, nothing to see here!" After all, I had stopped drinking for months at a time when I was bodybuilding. I had the willpower to do it again.

And then there really would be nothing to see. I would be sober. I would be a good mother. I had been over-functioning for everybody else. Now I had a life inside me to take care of, and he saved me. It was like God gave me another shot, a chance to start over.

I took that shot. No one could have been more conscientious about prenatal vitamins, doctor's visits, proper nutrition, and birthing classes. I was on the mommy train. During my pregnancy, I actually picked up a few more clients who saw how well I was caring for myself and Xavier before he was born.

I asked friends and researched parenting, and I read diligently on how to be a good mother. Because of my checkered experience being mothered, I wanted to make sure I did the best for my son now that it was my turn. I studied for parenthood like it was a final exam in a class where I absolutely had to have an A.

The birth itself went as well as it could go. Sure, it was a kind of pain I'd never experienced before, a confusing, blinding, tearing pain. But it also felt like hard physical work, and I felt on sure footing with physical work. I could do that.

Mom, Dad, and Meredith stayed with me during my labor at the hospital. Chad came and went. He excused himself at one point to hit the gym, an absence my family found strange and upsetting. But he returned for the birth, and I could tell as soon as he laid eyes on his son that he loved him absolutely. Well, that was one thing at least that we would always have in common.

It would have been nice if the sobriety I embraced during my pregnancy for Xavier's sake could have extended for the rest of my life. It would have been ideal if I could have walked out of that hospital after his birth with a clean bill of health in every way. But that wasn't my story.

Preparing for Xavier's coming had been like scrubbing one area of a room while hiding the rest of the mess behind a curtain. That mess was going to come invade the clean places because I hadn't cleaned it up first. I was bringing my baby home to a messy life.

Here I had a child that I feared I wouldn't raise well. I had a relationship that was failing. I had a fitness business that took up all my spare time. I was working hard enough for three people without giving myself what I needed to thrive. What was I supposed to do but keep coping?

When postpartum depression wracked my body with conflicting hormones and shocked my psyche with anxiety and lethargy in turns, I came to Waynesboro with my newborn child. My sister and mother looked after Xavier and let me sleep. Nobody should underestimate sleep as a treatment for new moms. You can't hold yourself together emotionally when you're physically spent.

My mom and sister were also great at reassuring me about motherhood. They told me something I have seen often since then and which I firmly believe. Every new mother believes that she is doing a terrible job. All of us believe, when that warm little bundle lands in our arms, that every other mom knows more about babies and is doing a better job at raising theirs.

If I could tell all moms two things, it would be this. First, trust your gut. You know how to be the mother you are supposed to be. You have a north star within you that will guide you into doing what is right for your child. But you have to get quiet to see it, and you have to be bold and peaceful to follow where it leads.

Second, take care of yourself. Postpartum depression is real and devastating, and there is no shame in seeking medical treatment for it. But even if you don't have that crippling condition, you can create a number of its symptoms in your body if you don't devote time and energy to caring for yourself, not just your baby.

In becoming a mother, I learned over time that I could and would do anything, face any hardship for my child. It didn't happen right away; I still had some more hurdles to leap. But faithfully pursuing recovery showed me the power of mindfulness, of noticing my own patterns of thought and behavior.

Have you had a life-changing moment like this one? Have you passed through an experience which convinced you that you had no choice other than to do the hard work of healing? If you have, then you know the inner certainty about what you have to do. You also know that it's not instant. It's a day-by-day journey, and it's one full of challenges and setbacks.

Doing the hard soul work of counseling, journaling, and other forms of self-examination taught me that I was strong enough to handle my pain instead of hiding from it. I learned how to fight for my own welfare. And in learning that lesson for myself, I learned how to help others fight for theirs.

EXITS

After my son was born, I hit a series of lows. Each one taught me about something I had to leave behind. I knew what my soul needed, deep down at the center of me. Now I would learn to walk away from the behaviors that were not helping me get what I needed.

These stories are ones that I hope will help you find your own path upwards. Watching me walk away from self-destruction should shine a light on some exit doors of your own. What is no longer serving you? What do you need to leave behind for good?

Exit from Denial

My first exit from something that was no longer serving me was not an exit I took by choice. It was one that happened to me, and it was permanent. All of the sudden, I could no longer say that I was fully in control, balancing everything in my life.

That morning, I showed up to my apartment, where I lived with Chad. Things were not going well between us. The only surviving part of our relationship was our son Xavier.

I had stayed out all night, dancing and drinking with friends. When I showed up, not later in the evening like ten or eleven but the next morning, Chad naturally thought I had been cheating on him. But it wasn't true.

I was chasing human connection, running away from the darkness inside me, and using substances to do both. That night, I had been blackout drunk, in a state that prevented both conscious decision-making and memory of what happened.

So here I came home, wanting rest and a shower and something liquid. I felt dehydrated and just so tired. So much depended on me. I was a dedicated, scrappy entrepreneur living my dream of running a fitness business. I was also the only person providing income to the household. Chad and I were accustomed to a certain standard of living, and I had to meet that monthly total and exceed it to meet my own standards.

Beyond anything financial, I was responsible to keep up the appearance of having made good in the big city. My parents wanted me to be a success. My wellness clients depended on me to stay in peak physical shape. And my friends depended on me to keep all my plates spinning safely in midair so that when I showed up to be the fun one, they could have fun along with me.

Most of all, my son depended on me. Tiny, perfect Xavier needed a mother who was present and loving and able to provide for him. I had only known him a little while, but his need for me occupied a great portion of my thoughts.

I felt so much pressure just to be, just to get through a day, one hour at a time, in the way I had laid out my life.

That morning in the apartment, I had a halfhearted argument with Chad. Neither one of us seemed to care enough about our romantic relationship to fight for it anymore. We had backed off from each other, leaving our son in the middle, caught in the no-man's land of our distrust and anger.

I pulled myself together with my usual routine: shower, makeup, clothes, a prescription pill to deal with the postpartum depression, and a protein shake in a carry cup to keep me moving forward. The possibility never occurred to me that the alcohol still in my system from the night before could do nasty things when mixed with my prescription. I thought I was being responsible, following my doctor's orders and my own healthy habits.

I got Xavier ready, returning his smiles, kissing his smooth face, inhaling the clean, soft scent of baby powder. As I left home, I was struggling. I could feel something inside me straining to come open, spilling all my guilt and shame into the sunlight where everyone could see. I took a sip of my shake, closed the apartment door, and wheeled Xavier into the elevator.

Sunglasses hid my eyes, and I passed a quiet ride down to the lobby, exiting onto the courtyard. Medina's hair studio was just ahead, and I needed to get to Medina. I needed to focus on my stylist and whatever wild story she had for me this morning. I needed to feel her skilled fingers on my head and the warm water on my scalp. I needed to relax. Then I would be okay.

I walked up the ramp to the salon complex. Medina's space was near the front, behind a dark wood door. I knocked on it.

She answered, "Hey, Girl! What's going on? I got all your stuff lined up and waiting."

Then she looked more closely at me. I leaned down to unbuckle Xavier and picked him up. The smell of his hair was pure and strong. He seemed too innocent and fragile to be near me. I handed him to Medina.

"Watch him for me," I said. Then I turned around and headed back out to Wilson Boulevard.

Now, Wilson is not the busiest street in the city. The chances of my actually dying on this four-lane road through a wealthy neighborhood were not the highest. But who was thinking logically? Not me. All I knew was that I wanted out, and this looked like the easiest, most obvious way. I just wanted the world to stop and let me off.

Xavier would be okay. Everyone else would be okay. In fact, they would be better off without me. I was toxic. I was ruined, bad, and unable to do and be what they wanted and expected of me.

A hand seized my arm. "What are you doing? Girl, come on with me."

How lucky I was that a good, solid friend was there for me at the moment when life forced me toward the exit from denial! Yes—my life as I was living it was unsustainable. I was in a bad situation: failed romance, body pushed to the breaking point, soul straining with unseen secrets, and practical pressures of work and responsibilities draining the last of my strength.

But I did not want to commit suicide. I did not want everything to end permanently. What I wanted was rest, and I didn't know how to ask for it. I had been in denial: denying that I needed sleep, peace, affection, and relief.

This moment when I stepped into the street was me walking away from holding the world together with my own two hands. Nobody can do that. Not even one of us.

These places where we feel out of control and overwhelmed can be scary. We don't like feeling powerless and afraid. But if we listen, these places can be valuable. They can clarify for us what needs to change, what is not sustainable. When you hit a brick wall, it's pretty clear that you can't keep going anymore; you have to turn around.

Exit from Destruction

Medina walked me back to her salon. Xavier was on her hip, a warm bundle perfectly comfortable letting Medina carry him around. I would do the same, let her take charge. I followed, unthinking and uncaring—not really there.

She put him back into his stroller, where he stretched and made kittenish sounds. I watched him squirm while Medina, in the background, cancelled all her other clients for the day. "I've got a family emergency. I will call you to reschedule. Thank you so much." She said these words over and over again while I stared at my son, not able to care yet

about the money I was losing her or the damage I was causing her business.

"Come on, we're going home," she told me. "Can you
walk?"

Could I walk? I had walked here. Yes, I could walk. I
nodded.

"Get yourself up, then. Girl, I don't know what is going
on with you this morning. Let's go back home. I'll take you
home. That's it. Come on, honey."

Then Medina called Chad and several of my other
friends. At home, I went to the bathroom and called Mom.
"Mom, I don't know what's wrong," I choked. "Something's
not right."

I don't remember what she said to me. I'm sure she prayed.
We hung up, and I grabbed a wad of tissue to mop my face.

When I came out, I saw Medina hanging up the phone, and
I curled up on the sofa with my head against the arm. I sat that
way, letting time drift past me, knowing I was safe because my
friend was there. She, on the other hand, crossed and recrossed
the apartment, straightening the mess I hadn't noticed before.
That wasn't like me, to leave a mess. I was almost obsessively
clean. What was wrong with me this morning?

Then the doorbell rang. I heard male voices and the squawk
of a police radio, and I knew who was outside. Panic surged
through me.

"Dina! Don't let them in! Don't tell them I'm sick! They'll
take my baby!"

She shushed me, hand on my shoulder. "Boo-boo, we have got to let them in. You want to pay for a new door? It's going to be okay. I'll explain. Nobody's taking Xa-bay. I won't let them."

I concentrated very hard on looking normal and competent. When the police entered, I felt my heart going like a sledgehammer. I could feel the pulse in my ears. I tried to answer their questions, but I didn't do a very good job.

Medina talked to them for me, told them I had postpartum depression and was taking medication for it. She talked about my business and my preparation for a bodybuilding competition, preparation that included diet changes. I could hear her flirting. The cops must be handsome in that rugged Viking style that was her type.

I couldn't make myself see their faces past their uniforms. They were just bodies in black, and I was a very small, powerless person about to be parted from someone I loved. This was familiar in a way I couldn't acknowledge consciously. Tears flooded my eyes, and my breathing went shallow.

Mom had sent officers to do a wellness check. I wouldn't know for sure until later, but I knew in my bones this was true. She had no conception of what a police visit would mean to me, a woman of color. She didn't know what a police uniform had meant in my distant, subconscious past, and she didn't acknowledge the potential for harm and overreaction, potential that had been splashed across the headlines for years. In her mind, a police welfare check was the next rational step, and she took it.

When the police entered, I tried to answer their questions, but I didn't do a very good job. At this moment, when I needed practical help and warm reassurance, I was getting an extra layer of stress and adrenaline. I migrated to the balcony. I wanted air. I wanted out. I could feel the anxiety rising in my body, through my spine and my chest to zing in my head. If I had felt an inexplicable pull earlier to the street, I felt an irresistible one now toward the balcony. The police were not chill with that move.

Other people came. Chad came. I saw him holding Xavier. Good. At least Xavier wasn't going to someone wearing black. Things went dim as the panic took me, deadening my ability to respond, to notice, to care.

That was when the handcuffs appeared. Because someone outside the situation had introduced the law into my mental health condition, it became a legal matter. The police escorted me through the building, past my neighbors, people I had to live with, and down the elevator toward waiting cars with flashing lights. My anxiety became like a living thing inside me that I had to use all my effort to control.

That day was a confusion of nurses and doctors whose names and faces slipped through my awareness and back out again. A needle went into my arm, an IV. I was wheeled into different rooms for tests, where I felt the warm stillness of the CAT scan or the noisy stillness of the MRI. I obeyed, held my breath, held my body still. I had stepped off the world, just like I wanted, and I was in the space outside it, the space where I was just a body that wasn't working right. I went back to sleep.

That morning had already forced me to question the story I had been telling myself. I wasn't handling life well. That much was obvious. But that was only the beginning.

Waking up in the hospital after a full night's sleep, free of the substances that had altered my ability to think and choose, and away from relationship and client pressures, I knew that my impulses the day before had not signaled an end. They had signaled a beginning.

I had to start trying. I had to find my way toward change and health. It wasn't just the street or the balcony that had been acts of self-destruction. Denying my memories, piling stress onto myself, and acting out to relieve my stress: these acts were all destroying me. I had to stop reaching for destruction. I had to turn towards life.

Exit from Definition

When I woke up in that hospital in Arlington, I wanted to leave and fix things. I reasoned that I had lost control for a moment in time, but I could do better. As I walked out through the big, glass doors outside the emergency room, I thought, "I'm going to take care of this problem and keep everything else quiet." But how could I?

I was waking up to the same things that had driven me into a dangerous state of despair and unhappiness in the first place. I was still low on physical nutrients because of my bodybuilding competition diet. My body was still craving the substances I had been using to bring it calm. My hormones and neuro-chemicals were still fighting to find balance after childbirth.

I still had all the same financial and reputation pressures. I still had all my inner baggage straining at the seams. I was still the same person with the same problems, plus more now that I'd had an expensive ER visit and a day of lost work piled on the rest.

On top of all that, I was starting to question the story I had been telling myself, the story about competent Inez, powerful Inez, successful Inez—Inez who can handle it all and anything else you care to throw her way. I was starting to feel a fear that I was going to explode any minute now.

The hospital wanted me to try AA, and so that's one of the first things I did. I learned some valuable tools in AA that did help me when I was ready to face the pain inside me and deal with the reason behind my addictions. But AA alone wasn't the final answer for me. I found that out through trying it—and failing at it.

Going to AA was tricky for me. After all, entering the building sent me right back mentally to the time I had been there with my ex-husband, Brian. Back then, I had come as a spectator, a support, not a participant. Now, part of me desperately wanted help. At the same time, part of me carried that spectator mindset with me to this place where I should have been coming with my heart wide open only to receive help for myself.

In my area, not many women in recovery were coming to meetings at six in the morning. So, one of the groups I tried was largely male and largely military. That was fine; some of my closest relationships were with males: Dad, my brother, and my son. The male group recommended pulling yourself up by your own bootstraps. That wasn't bad, but I felt something was missing.

I later went back to groups that were mostly female and had a different experience. I got to know a lot of great people. These women were supportive and warm and wonderful listeners. Though they came from all walks of life, they accepted one another and spoke honestly with one another in a way that I wasn't used to hearing among women generally.

I could talk about postpartum depression, balancing work and motherhood, and the sadness and fear that seized me about losing my shape to pregnancy and struggling to get it back. I couldn't talk about these things at the men's groups like I could with the women. It was a relief and a comfort to hear them talk about similar things in their own lives.

But in all the AA groups, there was this common understanding of alcohol as a disease and an addiction, of alcohol as the main problem. When we apologized to people we'd hurt and made amends, there was this underlying assumption that we were different people before because alcohol was controlling us. Now we were not those people. Alcohol was the barrier standing in the way of a healthy relationship, and now that it was gone, everything was good.

I had a problem with thinking this way. I always understood that alcohol wasn't the only problem standing in the way of healthy relationships with the people around me. I couldn't blame my actions on this substance, or on my unhealthy use of this substance. It never seemed completely true to say so. I didn't point to alcohol as the reason for everything going wrong in my life, because it wasn't. I could not accept the narrow definition of me as an alcoholic.

One AA meeting in particular made things clear for me. Until this particular meeting, I had understood my drinking problem to date back to college, getting worse in my corporate years. But then I heard a man talk about drinking beer in second grade to deal with stress. Suddenly, I remembered the first drink I had ever taken. A lost memory suddenly reappeared.

I drank the first time as a child, the night of the rape. I drank to avoid angering the dangerous strangers around me. I drank to fit in, to disappear, and to hide from a situation that had grown way beyond my ability to handle it. Alcohol for me would always be linked first to trauma—not to stress or partying like I had thought. That reclaimed memory changed my view.

Alcohol was one go-to comfort I was using to deal with the unspeakable things inside me. I had other tools. Overwork was one. The more successful I was, the fewer questions people asked, and the less I had to think. Also, the more I worked, the more I deserved to party to let off steam. Physical exercise was another. It legitimately made me feel good, and it quieted my fears and anxieties, too.

Lots of people out there use different activities and substances to quiet their own panic. Some of these strategies and products are healthier and more socially acceptable than others. But when we talk about those unhealthy coping strategies, we have to acknowledge that addiction is addiction is addiction, no matter how it hides.

Addiction can hide in alcohol consumption and drug use. In our society, the milder forms of indulgence are just fine, even welcome. Look at wine moms, beer dads, and the stoners who are a perpetual joke in every other movie out there today. There are also love, sex, and porn addicts.

Don't forget money. It's a great releaser of happy chemicals, and several kinds of addiction center on it: overwork, gambling, and compulsive shopping. And there are people who use food as their drug of choice, either for what it does for them chemically or for the feelings it evokes.

I consider sobriety to be just one part of a complex experience. If you focus just on the kind of habit, you lose a level of power and understanding. Your addiction is not your definition.

The most important thing I can show you is that your main job is not to beat a habit. Your main job is to heal from the wound that drove you to that habit in the first place. Your biggest problem is your pain. And when you heal, you won't need the habit anymore.

Exit from Desperation

Chad and I had never been married. And because there was no legal contract beginning our relationship as partners and co-parents, there was no legal contract governing the end of it. So much of child welfare law in its practical outworking depends on the parties involved working peacefully together. Chad and I did not.

My relationship with Chad had started to go bad when I realized that I had become our sole support. He was lying to me about having a job when he didn't. Leaving me and taking me to court for full custody and child support was part of his strategy to keep him from being homeless without an income. I didn't know that until later; what I knew was that the burden of caring for the three of us was all mine.

Then Chad started to build a case against me. He started recording me; he started emailing and connecting with lawyers and collecting information he thought would show that I was an unfit mother. He contended that what made me unfit was my use of alcohol. By the time I caught wind of what he was doing, he was also able to add my trip to the psych ward to prove I had mental health issues.

With some distance and perspective now, I can say that Chad is a good dad, and there was some validity in his concern. Absolutely, however, I believe Chad attacked me with an ulterior motive. He fought the custody battle in a manipulative, narcissistic way. After all, you can do something for a good result and still do it with bad intentions.

Unfortunately, Chad had a better shot at gaining full custody than I did. There is a common belief that mothers always win custody. No. If there is any drinking, postpartum depression, or any other serious problem, a mother's custody rights are in jeopardy.

Our troubles with custody began the night Chad and I attended a gala. I pulled Chad to the side and asked him about his job. I had already spoken to his company and found out that he had been fired. He lied and got angry. Knowing the end had finally come, I took his key to my apartment—the apartment where I was paying all the rent. I picked Xavier up from Chad's sister and brought him home. I assumed Chad would stay with his sister. He was done living off me.

But during the night, Chad did come back. In the middle of the night, he showed up drunk and started banging on my apartment door. So that he wouldn't wake the neighbors, I let him in and let him sleep in the bed, while I slept on the couch with Xavier until my babysitter got there.

The next morning, I left the house to teach a full day of fitness classes, leaving my friend in charge of my son. Once Chad woke up, he told my friend to get out. Then Chad took what he could and fled back to his sister's house with Xavier. The babysitter called me and told me what happened. So, when I finished work on Sunday, I came to get Xavier back from Chad at his sister's house. And Chad called the cops on me.

They told me to leave without my son. I did not take Xavier home with me. That act of revenge for my confronting

Chad and drawing a line started a long, drawn-out court custody battle over Xavier. This battle brought me to desperation; I would do anything to end it.

When Xavier was gone, I missed him like a limb of my body. I could not bear being away from him. For Chad to keep him away from me felt like the worst thing he could possibly do. It was at this point that I hired a lawyer, and so did he.

Because of the law on possession and custody, there was little that my lawyer could do to compel Chad to let me see my child. But that did not stop me from asking. I hounded my lawyer, and we filed an emergency hearing stating why I needed to meet with my son soon.

Finally, the court allowed a visit. Chad's lawyer and mine arranged for Chad to come to a restaurant in our neighborhood. We met, and holding my baby felt like the first breath of fresh air after a room full of smoke. I could not imagine letting him go again. After a while, Chad got up to go to the bathroom. I pushed Xavier in his stroller out the door, heart racing and eyes leaking. I reached my car and put Xavier into his car seat.

But Chad stopped me, and he called the cops. Chad spun the cops a tale, and the cops listened to him. Sneakily opening my back seat while I was getting into the driver's seat, Chad unbuckled Xavier and took him.

The cops told me there was nothing they could do. For the third time, police officers helped Chad keep my son from me. There was no custody agreement. There was no legal reason for them to side against me. They just did.

Later, I did manage to get Xavier for a visit. But I was paranoid every moment that Chad would show up to grab him away. We had several exchanges, not as fraught as the one in the parking lot of the diner, but close.

The final encounter of this kind happened at a pediatrician's office for Xavier's six-month checkup. On this day, Chad showed up before I did in a suit (he was unemployed) and told the doctor what an unfit mother I was. By the time I showed up, I could tell that the staff believed him. He had the office in his pocket.

I had a friend with me because I was so panicked about the very real possibility that Chad could be anywhere, at any time, ready to take Xavier from me. If my previous encounters with the police had taught me anything, they had taught me that I needed allies.

I had to get some distance to work things out. I had to be able to count on seeing my son again before I could let him go. I had one chance to keep Xavier without losing him indefinitely to his father. To keep custody for the time being, I had to run with him.

When we got into the exam room, my friend looked at me and said, "I've got the stroller." That was all I needed to hear. We both started running. I clasped my baby safe to my chest and dashed out of the doctor's office. I got down the stairs and out the door, and I ran half a mile straight down Fairfax Drive. Reaching my apartment, I grabbed a few things and drove away.

I went home to Waynesboro, and then I contacted my lawyer to make a permanent, binding, fair custody agreement. While I had the power to act, I would end this time of desperation. I would remove this state of emergency so that I could focus on my own healing.

Exit from Dissociation

Gradually, I began to learn what I needed to do to change my reality. This education happened slowly. Sometimes I was forced into the knowledge, and sometimes I felt ready to face it. It came to me through therapy, through revelation, and through experience. But I can say that my particular education changed me.

Because I understood better as an adult how limited the worldview was that I had trustingly accepted as a child, I read different views of history, philosophy, and religion from a wide variety of perspectives. I wanted to hear all the voices, all the experiences, not just the mainstream. As a person of color, it was my duty to learn the truth and voice it.

My struggle to learn and to improve myself took years. I can't point to one moment and say, "This is where everything changed, where I learned the one secret that solved all my problems." No. Some lessons I learned as a child, and some I am still learning. The habits of reflection and authenticity that finally enabled my life to change were ones I learned by doing in the years after I claimed sobriety for the last time. But they were built on lots of practice, lots of failure, and lots of learning.

My friend Tim, a pastor in the D.C. area and a fellow graduate of the University of Lynchburg, was a big help. I was desperate for direction, for someone to tell me how to be happy again. And as soon as I sat down to lunch with him one day, I knew he could help me.

Because we hadn't seen each other in a while, Tim started catching me up, talking to me about his wife and kids. Their life wasn't perfect—he shared some struggles—but he spoke with real warmth and respect and fondness about his family. His eyes lit up.

I wanted so desperately to have what he had. I asked him how he had managed it and how I could get that kind of genuine happiness, too. And thus began a years-long spiritual friendship that has meant a great deal to both of us.

Building on my already-present physical discipline, Tim challenged me to go back to Scripture. Just read the words and take them seriously. Ask questions about them. See where I could apply some bit of wisdom or advice. He invited me to Bible studies at his church.

The habits Tim encouraged me to develop did help me. I found guidance in Scripture, a source I had not consulted in a while. But the greatest gift Tim gave me was the assurance that God loved me.

God was for me; he accepted me. And no huge screw-up on my part was going to drive him away. He would keep reaching for me, trying to communicate with me, as long as I lived. I could not possibly run out of chances to feel and understand his love.

Tim's influence gave me hope in a very dark place. He was a brother to me when I needed one. I will always be grateful for his encouragement to pick myself up and keep going.

I needed that encouragement because this entire period felt like a very dark time. Healing is not for wimps. Looking at all your worst memories and all the shame and regret you've refused to examine causes its own pain.

One place I learned to open my heart and look inside was in therapy. I came to therapy for the first time when I was still in that on-again-off-again place of not knowing whether I actually could stay sober permanently. So, when I began seeing Dr. Wolfe, I only circled the truth without doing the real work.

Only when I had come face to face with the last test I could handle did I return to her ready to do what I was going to have to do. (I'll talk about that test later.) In her meetings, she and I examined the painful and shameful things inside me, one by one. Some of the things, I could just tell her. I could journal through those surface memories.

But some things I had buried for so long that I honestly could not recall them when I tried. They were like black holes in my soul: still exerting a terrible, destructive gravity on me even though they were invisible. When I would try to answer a question or think about why I felt a certain way or harbored a certain fear, my soul skittered away from that dangerous territory.

Going to a licensed, professional therapist is extremely important, in part because of the skill and training that licensure requires. There is no way that a friend, relative, or concerned amateur would know how to work loose a dead memory without harming you in the process. Dr. Wolfe knew how to reunite body and soul to bring these experiences to life.

She and I worked through techniques like EMDR (eye movement desensitization and reprocessing), in which she would guide my eyes in rhythmic motions that allowed me to recall the facts of an experience at a safe distance from the traumatizing emotions. We also used brainspotting, another eye motion technique that links eye position to memory to aid processing. Dr. Wolfe continually amazed me with the ways she knew to provoke my heart and soul gently and intelligently to reveal what had been hidden inside me.

These kinds of techniques are a real gift. If therapy doesn't seem to be helpful, it could be that the root of the issue is hidden from you. A licensed professional can access different techniques to help us know all of what we need to examine and address.

I came face to face with a lot of horror, shame, hurt, and disappointment in Dr. Wolfe's office. I remembered the rape for the first time since it happened. I learned that I could tell her absolutely anything without fear of judgement or disgust.

Together, she and I discovered the memories, terrors, regrets, and dread that I had to face in order to live fully conscious, aware, and in control of my reactions. She wasn't going to do the work for me. But she was going to stick with me while I did it.

When I took this exit from dissociation, I took away the power of these memories over my subconscious. They could no longer stress me out without showing themselves. And when I could look at them for what they were, I found that I was strong enough to deal with them.

Exit from Detachment

Another place I learned to face the past was with my friend Julie. Dr. Julie Lopez is a busy professional, a counselor who runs a wellness center focused on emotional and spiritual wholeness. Another friend had told Julie about me being adopted and some of the things I was experiencing. Upon hearing about me, Julie wanted to meet me.

She, too, had been adopted—not because her mother was imprisoned but because Julie was the product of a rape. Her whole life's work centered on addressing this trauma. She had even written a book about it, *Live Empowered.*

Soon after meeting Julie, I went to her wellness center to participate in an offering dealing with adoption. For the first time, I heard in a collected way some of the difficulties all adopted children faced. There were prayers and times for sharing and other guided activities that helped me feel in a whole new way like I understood what had happened to me as a baby and how to deal with it.

Intrigued with her as a professional and endeared to her as a person, I kept up my friendship with Julie. When we met one day at the Peacock Café in Georgetown, D.C., she invited me to join a retreat she had planned in Isla Mujeres, which means the Island of Women.

Isla Mujeres looks like a magical paradise without any worries. Most of the land is sparse and flat, open to sky and sea in a way that makes you feel deeply connected to both. Julie created a luxurious environment for us, booking a world-class resort and ensuring that we had fresh, appealing food ready when we wanted it.

I came to this retreat without knowing any of the other participants in advance. Julie knew us all, and we trusted her to put together a group of women who were all focused on rest, health, and connection. We did activities together in the morning, usually a discussion or an exercise.

But other than these events, all the participants could curate their own experience as they wished. I met dear friends at that retreat, Ati and Jen among them. They accepted me as I was, listened to me thoughtfully and kindly, and knew when it was time to go have fun. One incident with Ati endeared her to me forever.

A lot of emotions had been stirred up by the retreat, and I was already at a pretty tender and vulnerable place. On top of that, I was staying sober, and so I didn't have my Tito's to take the edge off and let me laugh at any irritations. One woman rubbed me the wrong way, and I felt attacked. Our interaction got heated, and I left, feeling raw, humiliated, and angry.

I went back to my room to take a shower, partly so that I could hide my tears. That bad exchange put me at the place where I thought seriously about changing my plane ticket and getting the heck out of there. Island of Women? Some women I could do without.

While I was in the shower, I heard a knock at the door. Then I heard Ati in my room, calling, "Are you here, Inez? Are you all right?"

Dripping wet, I stepped into the room, still sniffing back the snot and tears of my ugly cry. I felt rejected and unlovable and just plain sad. I was not all right. Ati could see my hurt.

Then she came and gave me a hug. I got her all wet, and she didn't mind. She held me, let me cry, and reassured me that I was still welcomed and treasured in the group. That hug was one of the single greatest acts of kindness I have ever experienced.

After that generous hug, I assumed I had experienced the point of the trip. I habitually distrusted women, and the hug and the way the group dealt with the difficulty helped to heal some of that distrust. But the trip was not done surprising me and giving me what I needed.

Here on this Island of Women, I decided to set aside Mom's Catholic ideals and trust the faith of my ancestors. The next day, I entered one of the rooms at the villa where we were staying to learn more about myself through the reading of tarot cards.

As I walked gingerly into the room, I felt a little wary. I saw an older white woman who didn't have a tooth in her head. The heat of the island had weathered her skin into worn, brown leather. My brain conjured every image of a witch I had ever seen.

I took a seat across from her. Not even looking up at me, she pulled out a bag of what looked to me like toys. She made a circle of many different statues or little figurines that looked like toy animals. I had no idea what she was doing. Then she started talking about my ancestors, and the more she talked, the more I just cried.

Suddenly, she made a statement that got to me. "You have a problem that's been passed down, and you have the responsibility to do something about it. This thing that keeps on being handed down generation to generation: you're struggling with it, and you're here to fix it."

This woman told me that I was in the circle of the figurines. As I was crying, I felt the exact same thing I had felt when the old woman had held my shoulders in the church in Cuba as I cried my tears of guilt over my marriage. I remembered and felt again that feeling of comfort and acceptance, and then the woman in front of me told me, "Your ancestors are here."

She showed me a rock. Then she put it into a plain, rectangular box, handing it to me. I sat stunned as she named the issues that the rock symbolized. Addiction. Alcohol. Pain.

She told me, "You have to keep the rock in the box and put it over there, because it can't be passed on anymore. This guilt, that shame that you're carrying, you don't need to carry it anymore, and you don't need to carry this to your son."

What a gift she had given me! My ancestors had each struggled with alcohol, with addiction, and with inner pain, and had passed that suffering on to the next generation. Now that the stone had come to me, I had the opportunity to hold it, understand it, feel the pain of it, and keep it from passing to my child. I could absorb the karma and remove it from my family line. What an honor it was to have that opportunity!

If we acknowledge our problems, then we all have this same opportunity. Only then can we keep from passing our wounds on to those we love, those who look up to us and trust us. As long as we hide problems from ourselves and others, we stay powerless to take them away. We have to look at the problem and say, "Yes, I do this; this belongs to me." Then we have the power to become free and to free others.

Exit from Drinking

For a long time, I thought I had things solved. There was a time before that morning with Medina where I ended up in the psych ward, and there was a time after. I was clearly a different person now. I'd addressed a lot of the sources of stress in my life so that I could handle things better.

I was going to AA meetings. I was seeing a therapist. So much had changed that I thought I had reached this livable plateau. Sure, I used alcohol every once in a while to take the edge off my stress or soften the sadness I felt when Xavier was at Chad's or when hard memories surfaced. But it felt like a manageable use.

The thing was that I couldn't possibly manage it. When I was blackout drunk, even if it was at a time when I had no responsibilities and was free to do whatever I liked, I turned into a person who couldn't make rational decisions or understand the consequences of those decisions. The part of my brain that understood, processed, and remembered just shut off.

Though I had made so much progress in my life, I was drinking in an unhealthy way. My romantic partner at the time had some unhealthy habits, and I chose to mirror his lifestyle and let myself relax and indulge when I was with him. Then something happened.

I faced a health crisis. It was something that blindsided me and took me to a place of worry and grief. Apart from any physical discomfort, facing this intense healthcare issue taxed me emotionally far beyond any other trial in my life. For the first time in a long time, I was in a life-or-death emergency.

Always intensely private about the things that felt most dangerous to me, I kept the details of my health crisis to myself. Then I entered a final period of testing to see whether I had recovered—or not. Medical professionals would need two weeks to read these test results and deliver the verdict.

During this two-week period, I traveled to Tulum, Mexico, a Caribbean city that showcased fabulous sunrises over stunningly clear, blue seas. Situated on top of ocean-side cliffs, Tulum was a historic site with temples and an ancient wall for defense coming from the rainforest. It seemed appropriate during this time when I was preparing for an attack from within to be here in this place of defense.

Also, the Caribbean felt like home to me, especially after my trip to Cuba four years before. The climate and landscape of Tulum felt Cuban, and the food and language recalled my homeland. People back home in Virginia might be looking at gray skies and feeling the bite of autumn wind, but I was walking on soft sand with warm light on my skin and ocean breezes in my hair. It was a comforting place to be.

Just as I had on those two previous occasions in the chapel and on the retreat, I felt that my ancestors were close by, just out of sight. I knew that whatever I had to face, I could face it with their help. I was calm, centered, and ready.

While I was waiting for news, I took a hard look at myself. Could I really still say that my drinking was under control? What if my occasional hard drinking was messing with my health? No one knew for sure what had caused my health crisis, but surely my alcohol consumption wasn't helping me be healthier. And beyond any physical effects, look at the way my blackouts had put me into dangerous situations over and over again throughout my life. How could I trust myself ever again while I was out of control?

Clearly, alcohol was no longer serving me. I had allowed it to remain in my life like a snake in a cage, not understanding its potential to escape and wreak havoc. Why was I keeping it around? Did I so desperately need those periods of oblivion that I could risk the possible damage to my health and reputation and relationships? What was keeping me from taking that final step and getting rid of that snake once and for all?

Past failures—certainly they were keeping me from declaring myself free from drinking forever. What if I made this big decision and then didn't follow through? What if I gave people another disappointment to hold against me?

Then there was loneliness. I relied on alcohol to make a space for me, to forge connections with others, and to allow me to be myself without fear of judgement or rejection. I would always need human connection. What if I couldn't find my way to it without alcohol?

And let's not forget white-knuckle fear. I'd started doing the work to understand and free myself from past trauma. What if things got too hard at a time when I didn't have this substance to help me numb the difficult feelings? What if my grief and anger overwhelmed me? What would I do?

Sitting with these questions, clear-eyed for the first time in weeks, I felt for answers. Yes, I might fail. Yes, I might be lonely. Yes, I would definitely feel all the desperate, gut-wrenching, heavy emotions that I had been putting off for decades.

But if I did not draw this line in the sand for myself and say no more, what else was I inviting to stop me? What outside consequence would magnetically find me and slam me to the ground, unable to recover? What would I lose if I failed to choose differently in this moment than I had ever chosen before? Would it be my child? My health? My work? My life?

While I asked and answered these questions again and again, I heard from my doctors. I was spared! I was not going to have to endure the hard road of treatments and side effects that I had anticipated. Best of all, I was going to live. What a relief!

That relief showed me something. I did value my health and my life, maybe even more than I had realized. And that value was incompatible with consuming alcohol ever again. I would stop. I would never take another drink again.

And I never did.

Exit from Distraction

However, my decision never to drink again did not sprinkle magic fairy dust over my life and erase every problem I had ever faced. I was free from a future marred by alcohol. But I was not free from the past.

All the potential outcomes I had weighed in Tulum as I waited were mine now to manage. Failing? I had to face that possibility daily. Managing loneliness and anxiety? I had to present myself to the world now with no aid from substances. Ghosts from past trauma? I had to learn to live with them instead of using alcohol to pretend they weren't there.

And in the middle of learning to live in these difficult new ways, I had an intimidating challenge to face—me and the rest of the world. Covid hit, and now I was trying to stay sober in the middle of a pandemic, when all routines were disrupted, all public meetings cancelled, and most avenues of support disappeared.

I was already dealing with the pain of being sober, and it was a pain. Memories were surfacing in therapy, memories that had been buried and leaking sadness or anxiety for years, and now I had to manage the pain of excavation, the pain of knowing, with no help from a substance. It felt sometimes like the memories were jellyfish dangling from the ceiling wherever I went, and I'd have to push them aside, feeling them sting, just to do any normal thing.

To handle the pain, I relied on the tools I had. One of my tools was physical exercise—running, lifting, stepping, dancing. I did them all. They helped center me in my body when my mind was shrieking in circles. Another tool was meditation, another really great way to quiet the mind. I went ham on self-care, the real kind. I diffused oils, prepared my meals in advance, took baths, went swimming, made nice coffees and teas for myself, and did every single thing my therapist asked me to do. I wrote pages upon pages, talked myself blue, filled out workbooks, and said mantras.

And here is what I learned. I have started walking a road that has no end. Yes, there are places to rest, and I'm not racing anyone. But I will always be walking.

In recovery programs, you introduce yourself by saying, "Hi, I'm Inez, and I'm an alcoholic." Everyone says this every time. But I struggle saying that I am an alcoholic in that way—present tense. I struggle with keeping that label in place on myself.

I don't think that I ever was an alcoholic, meaning that I don't think that I was someone for whom alcohol was the main problem. Pain was my main problem. Alcohol was, for me, just a toxic distraction from the main problem.

I was an unhealthy, unhappy person coping with trauma by using alcohol. Now, I'm not using alcohol as a coping mechanism; therefore, I am not an alcoholic. And drinking is not something I miss. Alcoholic beverages are not a temptation for me.

Numbing out and not doing the work? Yes, that's a temptation. Sometimes you get tired of doing the good things, over and over. I crave rest and relief, but I don't necessarily drool over a glass of wine or a bottle of vodka.

We turn to our coping mechanisms because they do something for us. They distract us from our inner pain. Sometimes when things feel like too much, we all feel like we need something to make the pain stop.

But coping mechanisms are flimsy. They don't do a good job for long. It's like we're walking on hot pavement. Our feet feel like they're on fire! So, we wrap them in newspaper. That's not going to last long!

Tools are like a pair of good shoes. They really do protect us while we move forward. They don't make the hot pavement cool down. But they do make us able to stand it.

Find your tools. You can use mine! Exercise, therapy, self-care, and talking to people who love you are all great tools. Maybe you use some others.

When alcohol does occasionally look tempting, I remember my health crisis. I remember the terror over losing my life, causing pain to the people who love me, and never seeing my child grow up. If that terror has been good for anything, it has been useful as a wall of fire between me and any alcohol. I never want to face the possibility of that kind of loss again.

That crisis was my final fall. My sobriety was my moment of resurrection. Since that decision, every step has led me upward. Every choice has been another chance to rise.

Exit from Disguise

When I had made it through a whole year of sobriety, I realized that the anniversary was going to pass without much fanfare. All of those years when I had been attending AA meetings, I had seen people receive chips for accomplishment. You stack up so many days or months or years, and you get a chip to mark that milestone.

But I was celebrating this anniversary in the middle of a worldwide pandemic. How was I supposed to say, "I did this! For three hundred sixty-five days in a row, I chose me. I did the work. I made it!" I wouldn't get a chance to tell my story. I wouldn't get a chance to say how grateful I was for this change in my life.

The pandemic had changed how I did business, as well. Sure, I had always had an online component to FitNez, ever since I started and built my own website. But I learned that virtual coaching was going to have to become a much larger part of my work.

I redesigned the user experience for my clients. I took classes and did research on interpersonal communication so that I could recognize non-verbal cues and read into facial expressions much more easily. I thought deeply about how I could show my clients that I was both professional and caring.

In a time when the world was turning upside down, I needed them to experience FitNez as a safe and welcoming space where they could put everything else aside and concentrate on themselves. Though it was a different experience meeting online, I created a space where they could see and hear the authentic me. And in order to let people know what I was doing, I made a series of promos.

To film these onboarding videos for my super-virtual offering, I hired a photographer and videographer named Patrick. He did a great job for me. And while I was filming the advertisements I needed for my business, I couldn't help thinking about my one-year sober anniversary.

I had struggled in silence for so long. I was carrying so much, and I knew that I needed to let it go. If I couldn't expect the usual chip and chance to share, I needed to find another way.

When we finished the last spot, I made a request. "Could you leave the camera going, Patrick? I have this big thing I'm celebrating."

"Yeah," he agreed. "Do you mind if I stay? I just want to see what you've got."

"Ahh, I'd rather you didn't," I said. I hadn't prepared. I wasn't sure what I was going to say. I wasn't sure at all that I'd be able to say anything.

"Well, it's a new camera," he said. "I just want to stay to make sure it doesn't mess up on you."

I kind of knew what he was doing. The camera couldn't be that faulty, right? I think he wanted to offer some moral support or some focus for me.

I took a deep breath and gathered my thoughts. What if this was an AA meeting? What if this was the one-year celebration I had wanted to have? If I was there, standing in front of my family and friends and fellow AA members, what would I say about the last year?

I didn't know what to say. And that's where the video started that Patrick filmed for me, with me saying, "I don't know where to start." Then I just concentrated on honesty and gratitude, and I let myself speak from the heart.

After I finished speaking, Patrick edited my story to show old family pictures and pictures from my adult life—pictures that showed all the parts of my story that I was sharing. Then I put that sharing out into the world.

The response I got was mixed. Some people contacted me that I hadn't seen in years. Debra messaged me and encouraged me as kindly and generously as only she could. I got messages from so many people, congratulating me on this huge accomplishment.

Some people just focused on the sensational confession that I, a professional fitness coach, had struggled with drinking. They looked past the point that I felt was most important.

The drinking was a secondary point. The whole message was that I was a wounded person. I had been in pain, and I had hurt people when I was in pain. The person I hurt the most was myself, and one of the ways I hurt myself was using alcohol to cope.

But I felt that I finally got to tell my story. I told the world that I was in pain and that I had used drinking to deal with my pain. Admitting that inner pain felt huge to me.

Even if I wasn't going to get a one-year chip at a meeting, I had shared the truth about myself. For the first time, I was appearing to the world without a disguise. I wasn't trying to be fun or competent or amazing. I showed my heart. I showed my scars.

Releasing this video was necessary for me. I knew how important the support of other people was to me. Without them, my heart wouldn't receive what it needed at this important time in my life. Starving my heart would cause me pain and suffering. And what had driven me to drink in the first place? Inner pain and suffering.

Filming what I did was my way of doing an end run around the pandemic. I knew myself, and I knew what I needed. I needed to tell the truth, and I needed to feel love and support. No world shutdown was going to keep me from doing what I knew was good for me.

How has the pandemic affected your mental health? Have you had to postpone or cancel things that feel necessary to your mental health? I'm sure you have. Let me encourage you to get creative about your needs.

When we say, "Oh, I'm okay. Nobody needs to show up for me. Don't make a fuss," we're usually wearing a mask, and not the kind recommended by the CDC. We're wearing a disguise that covers not our faces, but our hearts. And those kinds of disguises only make things worse.

Speak up for yourself. Say what you feel. Do what you need. That's the way to true health.

ZONES

Living a mindful, peaceful life takes a lot of balancing. Even though I'm sober now, I still have to work at my health and sobriety. After all, I will always have childhood trauma inside. I still have hard places in my family relationships. And running a business will take a great deal of effort and energy from me as long as I do it.

But life is a gift. Mine is, and I know yours is. How are you taking care of that gift?

I've found a way to help me balance the zones of my life that need care. When I see an issue, I know that I need to pay more attention to one of these zones. They are the mind, body, heart, and spirit.

Below, I've outlined principles for each zone that help me keep myself together. These twelve principles have guided me into a way of life that is sustainable, fulfilling, and peaceful. By thinking them through and adopting them, I hope that you will find a path to balance and health for yourself.

Mind

The three areas in your mind zone are your discipline, curiosity, and discernment. Discipline is the engine to your achievement. Curiosity keeps your interest going toward all those new areas you want to explore. And discernment helps you figure out what's good for you and what's not.

Children and young adults have school to help them tend to the health of their minds a lot. But as adults, we often let our minds have an extended vacation. Work is hard, right? Don't we deserve to relax when we're not there?

Our minds are valuable tools. And training them benefits us in ways beyond just our careers. We still have so much potential! Do you want to learn a second language? Explore a different religion or a different culture? Learn a practical skill like woodworking or knitting? Get into a sport like squash or sailing or skateboarding? Your mind is capable of all these things and more when you learn to engage your discipline, curiosity, and discernment.

Discipline

In the process of writing this book, I've asked my friends and family and clients what they perceive about me that makes me able to stick with sobriety. Almost without exception, they've told me, "Well, you're one of the most disciplined people I know." In fact, listening to them, you'd think that you could throw out every other positive habit and only stick with this one.

I can see why people would think that. Discipline is super important. It's the drill instructor inside you that bangs trash can lids together at zero dark thirty and tells you, "Get up! You said you had goals! Let's get cracking, sunshine!" You just don't get far without listening to your drill instructor.

What was vital for me was inviting my drill instructor to manage different areas of my life. I'd always been able to count on him to scream at me when I was preparing for a bodybuilding competition. "Get out of bed and get your butt to the gym! Don't you dare order that fried chicken! No Tito's when you're training!" He was good like that.

But I'd never thought to let him into some other important areas, like setting healthy boundaries with my friends and family, reserving the first minutes of my day for meditation, or eliminating negative self-talk. It turns out that he was pretty great at tending my mental, emotional, and spiritual health, too, not just my workouts and eating habits.

Your life will change when you make friends with your drill instructor. Sit down with him and tell him what's really important to you. Invite him to stop you from dwelling on painful memories, hanging out with people who aren't good for you, or wasting your time on what doesn't serve you. Then listen to the guy. He yells because he cares.

Curiosity

When you're raised in a strict childhood home like I was, you can feel like your curiosity doesn't thrive easily, especially regarding the big questions. They feel more like big statements, really—ones you memorize and repeat until your brain turns mushy. Your teachers and religious leaders present you with a view of the way the world is and encourage you to accept it.

Since I've become an adult, I've learned the value of curiosity. I love to hear different thinkers and learn different ways of viewing the world and its history. Curiosity has led me to understand more about what I value and why I believe as I do.

Curiosity leads to other great benefits, like creativity. Your brain unlocks when you ask it "what if?" You can approach problems calmly, expecting an answer, when you leave the question open-ended that way.

It has also made me a more positive person. Instead of feeling like a soldier defending some fragile tower of truth, I feel like a fellow traveler, happy to hear stories from the road. I see what I can learn from the people I encounter instead of feeling like I always have to be the teacher.

Being a mother teaches me every day about the value of creativity. I look at the way Xavier approaches the world with such fascination and wonder, and it makes me want to look at things that way, too. One of his favorite questions is, "What's that?" and another one is "Why?" He loves to find out about what surrounds him. I learn from him to look closely and to ask about what I don't know.

Here's another way curiosity is valuable. It allows me to participate in self-examination in a constructive and positive way. I can look at parts of my life and ask, "Is this serving me?" I should never have to get to a moment of crisis to decide to stop a habit or a relationship. Even if something is not a problem for anyone else, if it's a problem for me, I should feel the freedom to identify it early and eliminate it.

Another great question I ask myself is, "What does this mean?" If I notice that I'm drawn to a particular person or activity or podcast or anything else, I can ask myself, "Is this desire leading to something else that I desire more?"

Examining my feelings about my corporate work environment would have helped me back then. I could have asked, "I'm choosing to spend my lunch teaching class. What's that about?"

I needed to be in the fitness world helping other people. That's what my spirit truly desired. Dissatisfaction was pointing me to ask myself what I deeply wanted to do and to be.

Discernment

And I balance that open-mindedness and positivity with discernment. When you're in the habit of accepting truth as prepackaged from a higher authority, you tend to accept that higher authority without question. But approaching the world with curiosity means that you're going to learn a whole lot of things from a whole lot of different people. You learn to keep what's valuable to you and let the rest go.

Take spirituality, for instance. I consider myself a spiritually open Catholic. The traditions of my childhood still hold great meaning for me, as does my relationship with God, who is always there for me. Remaining spiritually open and curious means that I encounter some faith traditions or beliefs that are not for me. That's fine. I don't have to incorporate them.

But when I was presented with a different spiritual tradition at the retreat on Isla Mujeres, my discernment recognized truth. Being curious led me to that experience. Discernment allowed me to receive that meaningful message for myself.

I trust my mind, my spirit, and the connection I have with God to tell the difference between what adds to my knowledge and my worldview and what doesn't. I also trust my education and my logic.

There is no human on earth, no matter how honored or in what position, who deserves my unquestioning faith. But the world is open to me because I trust my discernment. What about you? How open is your world?

Body

The three body zones are nutrition, exercise, and hydration. Each of these areas is so important that we can't neglect even one. Your body works together as a single organism. Neglecting one part of this zone will throw the whole organism out of whack.

If you're starting from ground zero, take baby steps. Don't expect to go from someone who's mostly inactive to someone who can handle a hardcore workout or a marathon in just a few days. Do one thing daily in each area to improve. Add some water. Add some activity. Make a healthy swap at the grocery store. You can do this!

Nutrition

You knew this section was coming up somewhere in a book by a wellness coach, right? You were right! What we put into our bodies is so important. It balances in such an intricate way with what we do that we can't afford to ignore it.

And beyond just eating for fuel or vitamins, eating mindfully can tell us a lot about our inner lives. Reaching for a comfort food or a favorite treat can serve as a signal for what is going on with our emotions. Is the pizza just a pizza, or is the pizza your chosen remedy for stress, sadness, boredom, or anger? If you choose to look at why you're inviting specific foods into your body, you can gain information that can help you achieve wholeness.

I have clients who will come and see me for a check-in looking like a dog who ate its owner's shoes. So much angst and guilt! That's never a healthy attitude to maintain around your nutrition choices.

Many times, my role as a coach is to unravel those choices and take the shame away from them. If you understand why you're reaching for something unhealthy, you gain power to make a different choice next time. I also help clients understand that they need to step back and gain perspective. One emotional choice doesn't undo a whole week's worth of planning and faithfulness. Progress is the point.

And I love celebrating with clients who work their plans and see success. Cheering them on brings me such deep inner happiness. Eating mindfully can be really hard for people, but it is so worthwhile when they master it!

Let me ask you: is it easier to save money or to spend it? It's easier to spend! We know that. In terms of nutrition, eating well is like saving your money. You eat all day; you work out maybe two percent of the day. Which one do you think is going to net you more results?

Hydration

Have you seen the meme about drinking water?

My Body: I'm so thirsty. I really need a glass of water.

Me: Okay. Here's a donut.

It's funny because it's true. Your body needs water to run properly. It's constantly reminding you of what it needs. But we don't always hear what it's saying.

Being dehydrated can feel like being headachy or sleepy. It can feel like hunger pains. It can feel like itchiness, distraction, or constipation. (Oh yes, I said it!)

So, we treat the symptoms we see rather than the cause we know. We'll take an ibuprofen with a Coke, eat a snack, watch TikTok, scroll Instagram, put on lotion, or reach for a laxative. It's really a life lesson. We do this with emotional and spiritual pain, too.

We feel lack of connection, anger over injustice, or despair over a problem that seems too big to handle. So, we turn to drink, drugs, food, sex, or money to ease our loneliness and sadness. We're giving our hearts emotional donuts.

It's not what we need. And it's a perfect picture of the larger cycle of addiction.

Do yourself a favor, and don't make your body ask you for water. Give it what it needs before it has to ask you in some unpleasant way.

Exercise

I have a unique relationship with exercise. Movement has always come second nature to me. It's a source of joy. It's also something I can't keep from doing!

Sometimes people who don't naturally enjoy movement as much as I do can use my natural love for it as an excuse. "I just don't feel that way. It's hard." Maybe. But there are a few things to consider.

Living a sedentary life is so dangerous. Seriously—we're coming to understand more and more that it's as deadly as smoking and drinking. Being a couch potato can erase all the other good choices of a sober, nonsmoking teetotaler.

Also, lack of motivation is why God made your will-power! Your mind will always want to quit before your body has to give up. If you put your inner drill sergeant in charge, he will help you over the resistance to the point where your body craves the movement. This will happen—trust me. I've seen the change too many times for it to be a fluke.

Be adventurous! Find the kind of movement that feels fun to you. Think of what you liked to do when you were a kid. Kids love to get out and play. What did you do?

Maybe you try a dance class, a basketball team at a rec center, or puppy yoga (which I think would be tons more fun than goat yoga!). The point is that movement doesn't have to mean lifting weights or running. It can mean sailing, ice skating, boxing, or dawn Tai Chi. You can find what suits you, what makes you smile.

I do this! Yes, I love weights and running. I love toning my body. But I also love dancing! I've just experimented with learning surfing, and now I can do that, too! With each new skill I try, I find a way to benefit my body and bring me joy at the same time. What a win!

Heart

The zones of the heart are authenticity, security, and happiness. Through the hard and soft places in my life, I've learned that you have to live honestly. The alternative leads to too much trouble. But when you live honestly, you have to establish boundaries to protect your security.

And through everything, you have to pursue happiness. I firmly believe that happiness, true heart joy, is one of the points of being alive. And no one else is going to hand-deliver your happiness to you: no job, no partner, no lottery ticket. It's up to you.

As you consider each of the areas of this heart zone, think about your own life. Do you feel stress from keeping up appearances that don't match your reality? Do you go to your unhealthy coping mechanism because you just don't feel safe emotionally? Is your unhappiness leading you to discover a deeper truth about yourself?

Authenticity

During my worst drinking years, I lived with a lot of fear. I didn't want anyone to find out the things about me that made me feel shame. But most of all, I didn't want to live in plain sight of the truth within me.

You would think that resolving to live authentically would focus mainly on honesty with other people. But that honesty springs from truthfulness between me and me. Trying to hide terrible memories and emotions from myself was what really drove the cycle of addiction for me.

This truth is so powerful because it means I don't have to live in terror of breaking sobriety. I embrace the hard parts of my life now. So, I don't have to run from them like I did before.

One challenge I face with authenticity is my nature as an empath. I feel deeply with people, and my instincts tell me to present the side of me that whoever is in front of me needs. I am not being false. I just learn to prioritize the real me and not get lost in the me that other people want.

For instance, I might have to have a come-to-Jesus talk with a client who is wasting her own time by not following through. I am ruthless when it comes to honoring self-care! I might sense that she wants comfort from me, but I have to provide truth instead. Or I might have to ask for support from a friend when my memories and regrets get too painful. Instead of hiding my need, I have to find a person who can provide that human connection, because that's honestly what I have to have in that moment.

In one way, living authentically is easier. They say that if you don't lie, you don't have to have a good memory. In another way, it's harder. There is a reason my psyche chose to slam some feelings and events behind a wall. Facing them poses a risk and a challenge.

And being honest doesn't mean that I make every part of my life public. There are some parts of my story that I'm still processing, and some parts of my story that belong just to me. That's okay. I can be honest with others while keeping some things private.

What I can say is that facing the pain inside is worthwhile. I prefer not having to lie to myself, not having to distract myself or blind myself. When I do the work, I can look in the mirror with respect, and I like being able to respect the person I see.

Security

Living out in the open like that, though, you are vulnerable. Some people are looking for a place to hurt you, and when you live honestly, you're providing them that opportunity. Some relationships are just not meant to survive into your growth.

People will tell you whether you can trust them with your vulnerability if you just pay attention. When you learn who needs to be outside your circle of trust, you draw a boundary. You adjust your expectations of those people, and you limit the time and information they can access. Send them love and light, but don't hand them a torch to burn you.

I say this, and at the same time, I want to acknowledge that you just can't cut out of your life everyone who is not good for you. Maybe it's a family member; maybe it's a coworker or boss at a job you can't leave. If you have to coexist with a toxic person, then take action in the when, where, how, and why of your contact.

When: Your time is your own, and you don't have to allow everyone to take up unlimited amounts. Schedule time with toxic people when you are able to handle it. Then set limits. With workplace relationships, realize that not everyone in a corporate environment needs to like you. Get up and move. Think of ending an interaction like the Oscars playing the shut-up music. It might be awkward or offensive, but it's happening. The microphone is shutting off.

Where: Your space is your own. Draw boundaries of absolute safe zones where toxic people never come. And recognize, too, the power implied in place. Like animals, we all have our turf. Going onto a toxic person's turf limits your power. Meet in neutral spaces to keep your own space yours and to remove the home-court advantage from the toxic person.

How: You might not feel safe being physically near a toxic person. If that's you, choose methods of contact that employ distance: email, calls, Zoom. When physical proximity is unavoidable, remember that your body belongs to you. Don't hug, kiss, or shake hands with someone you don't choose to invite into your space that way. You don't even have to smile. Truly.

Why: Guard your why. A toxic person must have a good reason to request your presence. Decide before the request comes what is a good reason for you. Your holidays don't all automatically have to center on your family. A hint that someone misses you is a manipulation that doesn't have to result in your agreement.

Put your own mental and emotional security in first place. No amount of guilt, bribery, or other pressure should get you to put yourself in an unhealthy place. After all, you're the one that's going to have to do all the hard work of healing. If you can avoid hurt, then do it.

Happiness

One of the best things you can do for your heart is to pursue your own happiness. People think that choosing what makes them happy makes them selfish. But joy is a legitimate signal that you're doing something good. You become a much greater asset to others when you're happy, as well. People would much rather eat the bread of a baker blissfully living his calling than the bread of a frustrated mechanic fulfilling someone else's expectations.

And when we pursue happiness naturally, we can avoid altogether the substitution and addiction cycles where we settle for fake happiness. Pay attention to what makes your heart soar, and then do more of that. Find a way to include your happiness in your life.

My dear friend, Andres, has a cool job as an investigator. But he wanted to teach fitness, too. For Andres, happiness meant using his time to add another possibility, another avenue to happiness and usefulness. For months, he studied and read and practiced, gaining the skills and certifications he needed to become a wellness coach. Today, he coaches and trains in addition to investigating, and he's living a fuller and more fulfilled life.

My friend Azam, who is a phenomenal DJ? That's his side hustle. Orlando, my Latin dance instructor? He teaches at night after work. I took the curveball life threw me and started a whole new ballgame teaching wellness. Doing what you love in some way is something you can do.

Spirit

In the final and most central zone, the Spirit, the areas are connection, reception, and gratitude. And I want you to notice something important about each of these areas. They're all kinds of response.

When we deal with spiritual issues, we're dealing with something beyond all of us. The spirit is invisible. We know what we believe through following a faith tradition, reading a book, or trusting someone. Sometimes we see things we can't explain any other way, and those experiences add to our knowledge of the spirit.

But the spirit is beyond our ability to create and control. Recovery programs tell us to turn to a higher power—something larger and purer and better than we are. We are the recipients of what that higher power has to give. We respond to it.

So, in this discussion of spiritual things, we're approaching our higher power desiring a connection. We come with hands open to receive. And we leave with gratefulness for what we've been given.

Consider how these responses to a higher power tally with your own spiritual traditions and experience. What kind of emotion and belief do you bring to your current relationship with your higher power? Is that relationship helping you?

Connection

An interviewer once asked me my number one beauty tip. As a podcaster on beauty and women's issues, she was probably expecting the name of a skin care line or a home remedy for a particular flaw. But when I thought about what kept the wrinkles away, what brought light into my eyes, and what brightened my smile, I settled on the only true answer I know: meditation.

When I open my eyes on a new day, I literally hear a voice in my head saying, "Let's go!" From that point on, I'm rushing at top speed. But when I start that way, I find that I'm not doing any one thing particularly well. It's really important for me to slow down.

Those first few moments of your morning can slip away into the past or the future so easily. We think about our to-do list in the future, our regrets from the past, or the relationship problems in both directions that become unmanageable in the present.

For me, there is no substitute for meditation. Those first few minutes of my day, I close my eyes and let my inner self rise to the surface where I can see her and touch base with her about what is important. I take a few minutes to get quiet and still, to savor the peace, and to pray in the same way I would catch up with a trusted friend. That one habit does more for me daily than any other routine.

If my life has taught me anything, it's that I can't live in isolation. I need to know that God and my own spirit are connected and aligned to face the day. I need to feel that support in my spirit before I feel the ground support my body.

But spiritual connection is not just about connecting in this silent way. God speaks to us through other people, which is one reason why healthy relationships are so vital. The people around you who are living in tune with themselves and the divine often bring you the love of God in a way you can perceive.

God moves people to challenge you, comfort you, and rejoice with you. I know that there have been times I've gotten a hug from a friend that was a message straight from God—a message of acceptance and reassurance that I needed right then. So as simple as they may seem, interpersonal connections are an important part of an active spiritual connection.

Reception

When I was young, I learned to pray a few set prayers like the Our Father, and it was good for me to learn those models of how to talk to God. But the general attitude I saw in prayer throughout my church experience has been a kind of long-term negotiation.

We ask forgiveness for sins. We ask favor for the sick, the poor, and the troubled. We ask blessings for ourselves. And in return, we promise things like good behavior or more devotion. It's like we're trappers in from the wilderness, going to the only dry goods store in town to see what kind of supplies we can get in exchange for our furs. And to me, it feels exhausting.

A good reminder for me in terms of God and the spiritual realm that exists beyond our senses is that we can't really do anything to influence it. We don't know what lies beyond our lives. Our beliefs are just that: beliefs. Very literally, we take them on faith.

So, I have stepped away from that habit of negotiation in favor of a habit of reception. I accept that because God is God, he will do what is good. I can't change his mind, and if I think about it long enough, I realize that I wouldn't want to.

God and the universe have sent me deeply meaningful gifts at different times in my life, and I received them without offering anything in return. I'm meant to notice and respond with wonder and appreciation, like a child letting a butterfly land on his finger. That kind of attitude leads naturally to thankfulness.

Gratitude

What's the only proper response for an awesome gift? Thanks. And think about what happens inside you when you feel truly thankful for something. You get this warm sensation of love and tenderness inside you. You feel bonded to the person who thought of you and chose to bless you this way. Everything around you starts looking up.

Do you know what happens inside you when you approach God this way? You start noticing other gifts, like a trail marked for you. Even the hard places in your life start to spark some positive feeling. After all, each one shaped you into the person who's standing here today.

For instance, my two mothers feel like a hard part of my history sometimes. I can focus on their errors and the harm I suffered because of their choices. But I can also choose to approach them with gratitude, knowing that God put them into my life, even if I didn't understand why.

I'm grateful for my birth mother, whose bravery landed me in America. I'm grateful that because of her, I have a beautiful and meaningful Cuban heritage and appearance. I'm grateful that she allowed me to be raised in a safe home.

And I'm grateful for Mom for my adoption and for her faith. The life experience of seeking comfort in a church pew led me to my ancestor in Cuba. I'm also grateful that Mom chose to be there during my son's birth and when I was fleeing with him for safety.

Speaking of fleeing with Xavier, my relationship with Chad is another hard area of my life. We ended things without much peace or love towards one another, and his fight to take Xavier from me hurt me deeply.

When I feel irritated at Chad, whether justified or not, I have to choose gratitude for his presence in my life. He is the reason I have my son, the one person who means the most to me. So many qualities in my son, from his handsome face to his confident spirit, come from Chad. I can't cherish bitterness against the father without damaging my relationship with the son.

If I didn't cultivate gratitude in my spirit, I could sink into despair, resentment, and constant anger. That's not how I choose to live. So that's not how I choose to look at whatever God wraps up and puts into my life.

Respect

Balancing all four zones is a lot. Keeping in mind all of those twelve principles may seem like a lot, too. But it's really simple. It all comes down to one core truth: respect.

In working with clients now, I find that the number one thing I teach is not necessarily the mechanics of nutrition, like the food chemistry or biology. It's not methods of exercise, toning major muscle groups, and making the most of time devoted to movement. No—the most important thing I teach is respect.

If you respect yourself, you'll make the healthy decision for your body, your mind, your spirit, and your heart. Respect for yourself helps you form and maintain positive relationships with the people around you. So, for people whose lives are sending them signals that something has broken down, I know my job is to nurture that respect.

To illustrate what respect for yourself looks like, I'm including a few stories from my life. As you read them, I hope you'll consider the secret I've found for living with self-respect: keep your BACK straight. Be yourself, Accept responsibility, Clarify expectations, and Keep going.

You know what it looks like when your BACK is straight? You're standing tall, looking everyone in the eye. You're proud of yourself. You're definitely acting with self-respect.

Is your BACK straight?

Be Yourself

A little while ago, I began coaching a group of girls in middle school. They had developed some unhealthy habits, and their parents trusted me to speak into this confusing, uncertain, embarrassing time of life with some common sense and hope.

I wondered how to approach this new type of client, and so I asked Dad. "How do I coach twelve-year-old girls about fitness and health? I can't talk to them the same way I talk to a grown-up working mom."

He came through for me with some simple advice: "Remember when you were twelve."

That was hard for me. But his words prompted me to revisit middle-school Inez. I never felt safe in my own skin at twelve. I remembered the feeling of wanting to fit in, not wanting to draw the wrong kind of attention, and at the same time wanting to be noticed in a good way.

I understood deeply how that dual tension could affect you. You want to stand out, to be the best or smartest or most gorgeous. Those places in young life get awarded to so few. As a result, most of us become followers.

You want to fit in, and so you look to the other girls— or boys—to see what they're doing or what they're choosing before you make your own choice. This impulse can affect what you wear, how you choose to spend your time after school, and what you choose to eat.

So many eating disorders arise from kids sharing talk about expectations for their bodies. They gather these expectations from media, social media, and the world around them. And when they get together and apply what they've gathered, the results can be deeply unhealthy.

Maybe it's an impossible body image that leads to anorexia—refusing food in an unbalanced way. Or maybe that impossible image combines with a deep need for self-comfort through binging on food. Then we get bulimia—binging and purging. Or maybe those images just feel so out of reach that we give up on them in despair and turn to food for comfort.

Even when our skewed images of how a body should look don't end in clinical disorders, they can end in unhealthy places. Our needs to be liked and told that we're okay lead us to follow the crowd instead of following our hearts. But we all need the same reminder: be yourself. Be independent. Make choices without taking a poll first.

These middle school girls that I was coaching felt the same struggles I had felt, and so speaking to their desires helped me show them what would help them: self-respect.

If they cared about their own opinions and welfare and health, they would make wise choices, no matter the peer pressure. I just showed them how strong they were, how worthy of their own good opinion. I reminded them that it was okay to be themselves. Then they were able to follow a few practical tips to great success.

Isn't it hard to be ourselves when others don't receive us well? We come with a changed life, with a positive energy, and with a sincere desire to live in peace, and we find that the past is still present with some people. It is hard to stay authentic in those kinds of situations.

As part of my healing journey, I attended a personal growth workshop. The information and exercises I learned there made a huge difference for me. I met people who wanted to heal and live authentically, which was amazing to see. One woman, Kimberley, listened to my whole story with a lot of sympathy and grace.

She was with me toward the end of the workshop, when all participants did the same exercise: completion calls. We were all supposed to think of a relationship that was troubled and call the other person. These calls were supposed to enable you to say what was left unsaid so that you and the other person could become clear on past actions that had caused the relationship to become awkward or to deteriorate.

"I know who I have to call," I told Kimberley.

"Who is it? You have quite a story to tell. I could imagine a couple of phone calls for you. Which one do you feel like you need to make right now?"

"I should call my ex-husband. I messed up, and I hurt him. I'm a different person now, as far as I've come with doing the work. I'm at the point where I think I can be honest with him and tell him I'm sorry for that."

"Then go ahead and call. I'll be right here."

With a heart full of honest apology and goodwill, I made one of those completion calls to Brian. I brought him my authentic self, acknowledged what I did wrong, and told him that I was sorry. In a really hard and humbling way, I was one-hundred-percent myself.

But he didn't want to talk to this new me. If he wanted to talk at all, he probably wanted to talk to the woman I had been when I hurt him. He still wanted to be angry at me.

So, when I talked to him, he just wasn't receiving me. He was like, "Yeah, yeah. I hear you." But he didn't really. He just wanted me to get off the phone and stop bothering him so that he could go back to resenting me in peace.

I would be lying if I said that reaction didn't hurt me. At the same time, I didn't regret calling him. I had told him the truth and cleared the air. I had no control over how he received that honesty. And I didn't hear from him again for a while.

Then I put out a video. Remember that huge milestone for me of my one-year sober anniversary? I felt so profoundly grateful to look back on the struggles of the past year and see how I'd come through them stronger and more capable to handle life. I felt the need to share my story in a wider way, to let the people who knew me understand more about me.

Out of the blue, Brian commented, "Congratulations on your new lifestyle." Knowing him, I heard that comment in a sarcastic, dismissive voice. I felt that he was saying I was fake and that my changed life was temporary. That comment could have derailed me, once upon a time.

But I knew something he didn't know. I had put my real self, my real heart, into what I said. I was being myself, being authentic and honest. And in the end, that's all that mattered.

As adults, we still feel this pressure to please. Without even thinking about it, we fit into the culture or the family or the work group or friends around us. Just like our kids, we need to consider what's deeply important to us and be bold. We need to be ourselves—especially when it's hard.

Accept Responsibility

Here is an example from before my sobriety. Mere weeks before I made my life change, I agreed to a nutrition consult with my friend Julie. She was eager to experience my specialty, physical wellness, and to implement some good habits for her family.

She went shopping to get the items on the list I provided. She cleared her schedule and her family's schedule so that they had a good block of time on a Sunday together to do some cooking and meal prepping. Then she waited for me.

After she'd given me a good margin of time for traffic or any unexpected normal delay, she called me. I gave her some excuse about wanting to watch the game, an excuse she didn't believe but didn't choose to challenge right then. Then she and her family meal prepped their ingredients without the benefit of my instruction, which would have been helpful. When I was on point, my work was engaging, informative, and motivating. I really wish I'd been there to give them what I had to offer.

Julie waited a few days, and then she sent me a note. She told me that she didn't believe what I'd told her as my excuse, and she shared how hurt and disappointed she had been when I didn't show. But she said that she cared about me, and she was available if I wanted to talk.

I felt that disappointment deeply. It hit one of my tender places. At one time, that kind of failure would have driven me to drink.

Luckily, I had a history of being deeply honest with Julie about some of the deepest pain inside me. She had heard some of my worst memories, and she still chose to be my friend. So, I believed that I could fess up without losing her.

I told her the truth, and I apologized. I accepted responsibility for what I did. She thanked me for that. And then we worked through her disappointment and my guilt and shame. This was a pivotal moment for me. I was so good at keeping up appearances that I rarely messed up. I rarely gave anyone any reason to suspect that I was not okay. I ran in panic from the possibility that someone may look at me and see the truth of what was happening to me.

Julie's reaction to me pointed to another way of being. It showed me that some people, people who really loved me, might know me deeply and accept me in spite of my flaws. Julie's honesty and reassurance, presented together, was unconditional love.

And unconditional love was a powerful reward for accepting responsibility.

Let me show you one other example of what accepting responsibility can look like, an example from after my sobriety. I was on vacation at a resort with my son, and we were having a great time. We ate wonderful, fresh food, and we had impromptu dance parties after dinner while a band played.

We shared a sweet moment one night during our dance party. Out of the blue, Xavier tugged on my dress to pull me close to him. Then he whispered in my ear, "You're the best mommy."

I have to tell you, my heart almost jumped out of my chest. That kind of affirmation, after all I had been through during the dark days of the custody battle, meant the world to me. Xavier's heart and soul were just full and happy, and he wanted to share that beautiful feeling with me.

But there was a fly in the ointment of our sweet time together. Another party vacationing at the resort included a woman who reminded me of myself in a former life. As I watched her, I saw a painful reminder of what my life had been like before my moment of decision.

For two days straight, I watched this woman drinking at the adult pool bar and making a fool of herself. My heart hurt for her. You don't drink that heavily because you're making memories. You drink that way because you're trying to forget.

The situation felt tricky to me. I thought back to the time of the intervention my friends had planned. I was so wounded and tender inside that I couldn't hear any constructive criticism. It all felt like personal rejection to me.

At the same time, I knew that my sobriety put me in a unique position. I had done the work to heal from that kind of behavior and the pain that caused it. I was healthy and able to enjoy my life because of hard work, yes. But I had recovered also because people cared about me and loved me.

I felt that my healing put me under an obligation not to stay silent. I couldn't turn away and pretend that I didn't know or care what was going on. Other people could tell this woman to stop her behavior and be dismissed because they didn't know what her life was like, because they couldn't relate to her. But I could. And that shared experience pushed me to speak.

I pulled her aside privately and said, "You've been drinking in a really unhealthy way all weekend. I would hate for you not to remember this. You should slow down."

She huffed and puffed at me for daring to say anything to her. But I didn't mind. It's our responsibility not to let others harm themselves, especially when they think it's okay. I don't know if this woman will even remember that anyone talked to her. I hope one of her friends will.

If you see something troubling, something you have the power to change, then you should. It's amazing how life presents you with opportunities to do good. Especially in ways you've escaped or been saved, accept the responsibility to share your blessings. Share your truth. Share your low points and your way of escape.

Someone needs to know what you learned, what you know, what helped you. First, do the work. Then, share the light.

Clarify Expectations

Let me tell you a story about a gift of friendship I received unexpectedly. Every morning when I meditate and pray, I let my concerns rise before God. It's not a demand that he fix them. It's like we're both sitting at the edge of a pond full of bright carp, watching the graceful, colorful fish surface and dive again. We both just notice what's rising within me.

Sometimes what rises within me is loneliness, either the old childhood loneliness of feeling unconnected or an adult loneliness of not being in a relationship. Sometimes it's fear that I'll disappoint Xavier, that I won't know enough or be enough for him. Sometimes it's regret over past actions or words. Whatever it is, God and I watch those emotions and let them go.

One day, just an ordinary day, not a day when I was feeling especially alone or anything at all, a neighbor waved to me at the pool. "Inez," she called. "Meet Matt! He just moved in. He's your neighbor."

Now this is not a rom com meet cute. Everybody at my apartment complex knows that I'm kind of the mayor. I try to know everybody, and nearly everyone exchanges a word with me when they're passing by. I also still like to put together social events, just like I did in college. It's fun for me to create a barbeque or a shared dinner or just a time when people with kids around Xavier's age can meet at the pool so that our kids can play and swim and eat popsicles.

So, I welcomed Matt and his adorable daughter and hung out with him at the pool. We are very different people, but we got along super well. I could also see that Matt was quieter than me and that there was a lot of depth to him. I got to thinking that it would be a shame if anything got in the way of a truly excellent friendship.

So, the next morning, I got some coffee and stopped by Matt's. He opened the door, a little surprised to see me so early on a weekend. But he invited me inside and accepted the coffee.

"Look," I started. "Our kids get along so great, and I

really like hanging out with you. I just want to make sure we can just be friends, that there's no pressure on us to be anything else."

"Sure," he answered, looking a little puzzled. He had not made any kind of a comment or advance, and we didn't know each other well enough for him to just pick up on the fact that I wasn't reading into things.

"I'm just super honest. You can be super honest, too. I value that."

Over coffee, we cemented the friendship that I knew was starting with a really great talk. From that time on, we knew that we could speak openly with each other and that we could count on each other.

I would ask him for a favor, like receiving a package at my apartment or watching Xavier so that I could go to the gym, and he knew that he could ask me for the same kind of favors or that I would stop by with chicken soup if he was sick. It was nice for both of us to have someone close by to rely on for simple things.

But beginning our friendship in honesty has lent me some unexpected gifts. When I start coaching him without asking, Matt can gently remind me that he's not a client, and I know to stop the flow of advice. And when I'm troubled, I know I can tell Matt and hear the truth from him about whether I'm at fault or I'm overreacting or anything.

Once when I was troubled, over what I can't remember, I brought my upset emotions to Matt. He suggested that it might help to look up at the stars. That might bring me some peace.

I didn't know if it would, as that was not a regular practice for me. But because I trusted Matt and he suggested it, I took a blanket outside and lay down in the grass. I looked up at the stars and breathed slowly. I felt my frustration begin to ebb.

After a while, I don't know how long, Matt's voice came from a few feet away. "You did it," he said, holding out a blanket. "I brought this in case you wanted to try, but you're already here."

"That was good advice," I told him. "Come join me."

He lay down a few feet away on the blanket he had brought, and we watched the stars together. It was just a perfectly safe, peaceful moment at the end of a hard day. And it flowed from this friendship that arrived like a gift. All I did was recognize the gift when it came, like meditation in the morning, like a flash of gold underwater.

Can you imagine how this moment might have been ruined if I had not clarified expectations with Matt at the beginning of our friendship? And it is never too late to start this practice. When we can get rid of misunderstandings and cross purposes ahead of time instead of letting potential problems grow in the dark, all of our relationships will benefit.

Letting people know what you need and what you can offer is a sure way to show respect for yourself.

Keep Going

Because we all mess up sometimes, I want to encourage you to keep going. While I was writing this book, I went to Costa Rica to celebrate my sober anniversary. I wanted time to reflect on how far I'd come. I needed space to consider my life's meaning and purpose. And because this anniversary felt like a birthday of sorts, I felt that old birthday impulse to get on the road.

But I also just needed rest. To do the work of reliving your memories honestly is a tiring process, and I needed time away from it. For a week, I would tend to myself with sun, exercise, adventure, good food, and lots of sleep. That was what I needed.

My time in Costa Rica was also going to include surfing lessons. I was really excited about learning a new physical skill and increasing what I could do to relax that didn't include drinking. Learning in Costa Rica also meant that I would get to experience a famous area, Witches Rock, which appeared in the film *Endless Summer*. The rock juts up from the ocean at an angle, a single obstacle a good swim out from the coast, and it churns the sea into a foaming boil, like a witch's cauldron.

For the first few lessons, my fellow surfers and I learned the basics at a beach right around the corner from our villa. Everyone learning had varying degrees of skill, but the instructors made sure we could all catch a wave and stand up on a board before they presented us with the opportunity to tackle Witches Rock. "Here we go," I thought to myself. "Now it's real."

I came out in a boat with a bunch of other surfers and our instructors. I was feeling comfortable about my skill level and my preparation. Our instructors led a few people out to the rock and surfed around it themselves. When my turn came, I was eager to try. I paddled towards the rock and got to my feet. Then I fell.

When I fell, I felt the enormous force of the ocean tugging me down. I swam as hard as I could, managing to reach the surface and call for help. No one turned, and I went down again. Panic and the raw animal need for survival kept my arms and legs going long past the point where I was just exhausted. I was overwhelmed.

My air was running out, and my strength was gone. I sucked in water with the last air that I gasped. This was it. This was the way I was going to die.

Then a hand reached for me, and voices called to me. I was never so relieved before. An instructor towed me back up on a board and helped me to the shore. I lay down on the wet sand, coughing, gagging, and sobbing. I was safe. I wasn't going to drown today. I didn't want to move for the rest of my life.

"You ready to go back in the water?" my instructor asked.

I told him pretty forcefully that no, I was not ready to go back in the water, not now and probably not ever. He let me talk until I ran out of protests, and then he reminded me that I had to get back into the water to get to the boat.

The boat. No. I would walk back to the hotel through the jungle. Anything but drowning. But the instructor talked to me until I realized the truth of what he was saying. The only way out was through. It wasn't the first time in my life I'd had to realize that.

Shaking and terrified, I swam. My body was screaming at me to get out of the water, and my mind was putting up straight exclamation points with no words. I passed the rock and watched the boat grow closer. When I reached it, many hands stretched out to receive me. Everyone was in a mood to celebrate. I hadn't died, and we had all done something really hard and worthwhile.

"Let's pop the rosé!" someone suggested, and immediately the alcohol started flowing.

I wanted some wine! I wanted to check out and not feel the terror and despair that had washed through me as I sank. But I didn't.

What did I do instead? Instead of relying on a substance to take away the dregs of my fear, I sat with it and sobbed through it. I felt it all and let it ebb away. Instead of drinking to foster a connection with the people around me, I presented myself, honest and wounded and in need. And the people around me accepted me and welcomed me.

That was a powerful lesson. My day surfing taught me that I was strong enough to keep going when I was at the end of my strength, that I was vulnerable enough to connect with the healthy people around me, and that I didn't need to hide from whatever was going to happen to me in the future. I could keep going the way I was facing what had happened to me that day.

That realization determined the rest of my trip. The first thing I did was go surfing the very next morning. I got up at oh-dark-thirty, made everyone coffee, and marched out to the beach right around the corner from our villa. The waves that day were glorious.

The second thing I did was listen to the recordings of people from my past. They talked about my flaws and my good points. They shared the memories they had of me. I won't say that listening to those recordings was easy. I will say that it provided me with a good deal of clarity.

Like going back into the water, listening to those voices showed me how strong I was. Like the water that had entered my lungs, I could expel those bad feelings and leave them behind me. I didn't have to try to breathe around them forever.

This is my hope for you. Don't try to breathe around the pain in your life. Cough it out. Cry over it. Pray over it. Tell it to a good person. Paint it or write it or sing it or carve it into wood. And then leave it behind.

It will follow you. Pain is sneaky like that. You'll be doing just fine, surfing along with the sun on your back and the wind in your hair, and then it will pull you underwater, stealing your breath.

But there is a shore. There is an end to the ocean of your pain. If you keep going, solid ground is waiting for you, along with friendly hands and faces, fresh air, and a brand-new start.

CONCLUSION

When I stand on this side of my healing journey and look back, I feel several things. First, I feel compassion for the small girl who suffered abandonment and rejection so early and so often at such a young age. So much of the hurt in her life was not her choice or her fault, and I send her love.

Second, I feel gratitude that I am on the other side of my healing. I went through a lot of hard places, and some of them were my fault. I am grateful that I have grown beyond the woman who made those mistakes.

Finally, I feel hope that my journey can help others. Inviting readers into my shameful or painful moments is a hard practice, but I believe that it's worthwhile. Knowing what I'm choosing to face and how I'm opening my arms wide to life both despite it and because of it should encourage you to embrace your own life.

Believe me, I know how hard change can be. I know the frustration and despair that comes with failing at it over and over again. Sometimes it seems impossible.

Remember that tattoo I got when I finally made my decision never to drink again? I wanted to keep that vow in front of me every day. So, I chose the date and a saying: Fall 7 Rise 8.

I didn't mean that I had literally fallen from grace or from wellness seven times and this was my eighth try. I meant that I had fallen as many times as I was going to fall, and I had reached an end of falling. I had completed that cycle in my life. From then on, I was only going to rise.

My way out took me time. I had to recognize what I needed and learn to pursue it in good ways instead of with coping mechanisms. I had to leave behind what was no longer serving me, and I had to face my pain and my truth in therapy. Finally, I had to balance all the parts of myself to live in a healthy way, respecting myself. I had to keep my back straight and hold my head high.

Do you feel unworthy because of childhood trauma or abuse? Do you feel disconnected from the people who are supposed to be the closest to you? Do you harbor shame for an assault that you've somehow internalized as your fault? Do you struggle with some soul wound to the point that you use a substance or a habit to hide from it?

With all the gentleness in the world, I tell you that I'm right there with you. I know how that feels—like being trapped. And I know the way out, too. I hope that hearing how I found it and knowing that it's there will help you find it.

Come alongside me. I'm still walking this path, and you can walk it with me. You can do this if it's what you want to do. Nothing hard disappears, but you can manage it. You are able and strong, and you can make the most of your life.

Let today be your day. Reach out for strength to God and the people who love you. And then—even if it's the hundredth time, the thousandth time—rise up.

ACKNOWLEDGMENTS

So many people have helped me during the writing of this book, as well as before I started unlocking the puzzle of myself. I am grateful beyond words for the ways in which you all showed up for me at the right time and place.

First and most importantly, I am grateful for my family: thank you Michael Sobczak for being such a patient and encouraging dad; I am grateful to Barbara Sobczak and Barbara Valdez for the lessons learned from each of them; many thanks to Meredith Keppell for your love and help; thanks to Ronald Sobczak for always being there; and thanks from the bottom of my heart to my aunt, Leslie Dulb, for believing in me and bringing out my best self.

I owe heaps of thanks to the people who helped me to discover who I am and how I work: thank you, Dr. Julie Lopez, for your work on adoption and your personal support; thank you Dr. Carolyn Wolfe, therapist extraordinaire, for your patience and persistence; thank you Tim Grant, for your honesty and support; thank you Jerry Ward for helping me push my limits; and thanks to the whole AA community for helping me embrace truth and health, especially Heather Harrell, who honored me with trust and belief.

Throughout my life, I've been blessed with friends who embrace me like family: Jamie Crawford, you had my back and kept my childhood secrets, and I will always love you; Debra Freeman, we shared adventure and laughter and loss, and you are always in my heart; Ati Williams, you gifted me with the single kindest moment of human connection I have ever experienced; Jen Adeli, you are a wild, brave, warrior, and I am thankful for my connection with you and Hamid Adeli; Azam Mirza, you are my brother by choice and the best DJ in DC; Joy Mirza, you are my style guru, and I am grateful for your presence; Medina Heard, nothing heals like your laughter, and I will always be grateful you were there in my darkest moment.

Aaron Smith, I'm grateful for a friendship that outlasted college; Emefa, thank you for being there during some hard times; Kathleen, thank you for showing me my gifts as a person; Orlando Machuca, you are a joyful and fantastic guide to my Latin heritage; Victoria Monroe, I'm forever grateful for your wisdom and companionship; Terri Marshall, thank you for listening; Reina J., thank you for sticking by me; Stephanie Abraham, thank you for believing in me; Stephanie Stapelton, thank you for being a faithful friend; Matt Hildreth, no one could ask for a better neighbor; Andres, thank you for striving with me to become our best selves.

And I've been blessed along my publishing journey to meet professionals who helped me shape my story and say what I needed to say: Kimberley Collins, thank you for listening and showing me how to be honest with myself on paper; Sharilyn Grayson, thank you for your research skills and your help with editing; Drew Xeron, thank you for your amazing photography expertise; Karen Anderson and the whole crew at Morgan James, thank you for making the complicated smooth and for encouraging me all the way.

Finally, I am most thankful for my son Xavier. You are the light of my life, and you are the reason I have kept reaching to become better. Being your mom is the biggest gift I could have received. My gratitude for you comes with a prayer that you will start from this place I journeyed for you and fly to heights I never imagined.

REFLECTION QUESTIONS

As you read the following questions, you can respond in a way that feels right to you. You might like to journal your answers. Maybe you would like to use them as prompts to guide a discussion with a close friend or a counselor. However you choose to interact with them, I pray that they will help you think about how you can find the strength within to rise one last time.

1. How did people talk about your heritage in your family of origin?
2. What about your heritage makes you proud?
3. Does your name hold special meaning to you?
4. What central trauma entered your life without your invitation?
5. How have you been dealing with that trauma?
6. What quality in you protects you from trauma the way my hope protected me?
7. To what extent did you feel accepted and loved in your family of origin?
8. Were there any ways you felt different from the family who raised you?
9. Who made you feel special and wanted as a child?

10. In what ways did you feel some separation from your parents as a child?

11. Looking back as an adult now, do you see root causes for that disappointment and distance?

12. How have you seen those same root causes appear in your own life, ways that make you similar to the parent who disappointed you?

13. How did the place where you were raised affect your sense of self?

14. In what ways did you identify with the people in your community?

15. Have you ever felt different from the people around you?

16. What role did religion play in your early life?

17. How have your views on religion changed over time?

18. What do you know about faith that is absolutely true?

19. Did you suffer a defining wound as a child?

20. What thoughts or beliefs led to that wound?

21. How do you see that wound affecting your decisions later in life?

22. How did you receive encouragement from your parents?

23. In what ways did you feel rejection from one or both parents?

24. Can you look back and see a core belief that sabotaged your growth?

25. What good quality remains in your life today that someone affirmed in you as a child?

26. How did adults in your life recognize and encourage what was special in you?

27. Who is on your list of encouragers from when you were small?

28. How did your childhood friends supply a quality that you did not get at home?

29. Were any of your friend's parents especially meaningful to you?

30. What did your childhood friendships teach you about relationships?

31. What are some ways your parents failed you despite their good intentions?

32. Was there a time as a child when you hid something that harmed you?

33. Did you ever get into a situation as a child that later felt like too much to handle? What did you do?

34. As a teenager, did you ever get into a situation that felt too dangerous?

35. What forms did exploring your identity take for you?

36. Have you ever pursued a relationship that forced you to compromise your health, safety, or future? What did you choose?

37. Were your parents able to celebrate special events and achievements with you?

38. What was uncomfortable or disappointing for you about leaving home for the first time?

39. What did you think was wonderful about leaving home for the first time?

40. How did you handle the first real freedom you had?

41. Did you form habits when you first left home that have followed you today?

42. How did you see hurts from childhood surfacing in your first choices as an adult?

43. As an adult, what have you learned about your parents that has given you clarity about yourself and your childhood?

44. What qualities, good or bad, do you share with your parents?

45. What needs do you still have inside that you wish a parent could fulfill?

46. What have you traded to find success in your life?

47. Have you noticed yourself changing to fit in with the people who are part of your environment?

48. How has life intervened to stop you when you were out of control?

49. Have you found some discipline or practice that requires everything that you have to give, that pushes you to your limits in a good way?

50. What natural talents and abilities inside you might be pushing you towards this kind of activity?

51. In what ways might this healthy habit meet needs that you are meeting in less healthy ways right now?
52. What qualities are most important to you in a partner?
53. Do you show those qualities in your own life?
54. How are you doing at listening to what you truly need instead of what others expect?
55. Have you ever gone to a place where you felt more like yourself? Where was that?
56. Have you ever had a spiritual moment of connection that was beyond your explanation?
57. What does connection to your own heritage look like for you?
58. How have your friends helped you see yourself more clearly?
59. What habits or behaviors do you rely on to help you connect with people?
60. How successful are you at setting boundaries with your friends?
61. Have any of your coping mechanisms ever put you in real danger?
62. How do you respond to being disbelieved?
63. Gaslighting is when someone pressures you to accept a version of events that is different from the truth. Does anyone in your life attempt to gaslight you?
64. Has some relationship helped you find meaning in life?
65. What message did that person deliver to you about yourself?

66. What person is your soul anchor: the person you would face anything for?

67. Have you experienced a low point that let you know you couldn't continue the same way anymore?

68. How did your friends and family react to seeing you in that condition?

69. Was that moment your final low point, or was acknowledging your problems more of a gradual process for you?

70. Have you acknowledged your inner pain, the thing that drives you to find relief?

71. How have you been dealing with that pain? Would you say your coping mechanisms are serving you?

72. How sustainable are the ways you've tried to heal from your inner pain?

73. What situations in your life have brought you to the point of desperation?

74. How do you deal with feeling desperate?

75. If things are out of control right now, could you take one step to establish safety and end your desperation?

76. How do you relate to the concept of hiding from events in your past?

77. In reflecting on your own life, do you feel some anxiety that doesn't have an obvious source?

78. Have you found wise mentors and professionals to guide your healing?

79. In what ways have you felt disconnected from your heritage and your family?

80. How might connecting with your ancestors or your heritage enrich your life?

81. Do you sense an opportunity to remove a generational failing?

82. When in your life has an event or a crisis gotten so serious that you didn't know how you could ever recover?

83. What are you absolutely not willing to lose?

84. At what point in your life have you made an irreversible commitment to change?

85. How does it feel to you to think of saying goodbye to your distractions?

86. What issues will you still have left to handle when your unhealthy coping mechanism is gone?

87. What tools do you have ready to help you deal with the pain inside?

88. How friendly are you with your drill sergeant?

89. What is no longer serving you? What desires do your habits prompt you to pursue?

90. How do the things you feed your mind affect other areas of your life?

91. Are you satisfied with the condition of your body zone?

92. In what ways might your body be telling you it needs something?

93. How can you change a habit to give your body what it needs?

94. How do the people in your life respond to your search for authenticity?

95. What has been your experience with setting boundaries?

96. How free do you feel to pursue your own happiness?

97. In what ways do you feel connection to a higher power?

98. How have you seen divine presence at work in your life?

99. Where can you find gratitude in the hard places of your life?

100. What were you like in school? Did you stand out or struggle to fit in?

101. Has your role changed in adulthood?

102. How can you see yourself letting small decisions slide so that you fit in?

103. What has been your experience with confessing your faults and owning responsibility for them?

104. How do you feel about the idea that self-respect is the foundation for healthy choices?

105. How has your healing journey helped you act with self-respect?

106. What has been your experience with misunderstandings in relationships?

107. Have you ever felt that people expected more from you than you were able to give?

108. How comfortable do you feel clarifying expectations with friends and family?

109. What practices do you have in place for the times when you need a healthy rest?
110. How have you felt the world pulled out from under you?
111. What does it mean to you to keep going?

ABOUT THE AUTHOR

Born in Miami to a Cuban teen immigrant, Inez Sobczak was raised in rural Virginia by a white Catholic family. Her struggles with rejection and trauma led to years of battling an addiction that she hid behind amazing grades, popularity, corporate success, and physical fitness.

However, the balancing act grew too hard to maintain, and Inez found herself lonely, desperate, and afraid that someone would learn the secrets she had been hiding. It was a bout with postpartum depression and a life-altering cancer diagnosis that finally led her to confront a hidden past and cope with her inner pain. Through a hard process of growth, Inez finally reached the point where she could lay down her addiction once and for all.

A successful fitness entrepreneur for over a decade, Inez has brought health and sobriety to numerous clients. She has also won bodybuilding competitions, most recently placing third in her category at the national level. Today, Inez lives in the D.C. area, where she devotes her time to wellness clients, competitions, speaking engagements, and her five-year-old son.

A free ebook edition is available with the purchase of this book.

To claim your free ebook edition:

1. Visit MorganJamesBOGO.com
2. Sign your name CLEARLY in the space
3. Complete the form and submit a photo of the entire copyright page
4. You or your friend can download the ebook to your preferred device

Morgan James
BOGO™

A **FREE** ebook edition is available for you or a friend with the purchase of this print book.

CLEARLY SIGN YOUR NAME ABOVE

Instructions to claim your free ebook edition:
1. Visit MorganJamesBOGO.com
2. Sign your name CLEARLY in the space above
3. Complete the form and submit a photo of this entire page
4. You or your friend can download the ebook to your preferred device

Print & Digital Together Forever.

Snap a photo

Free ebook

Read anywhere